A Photo History of
TANKS
in Two World Wars

A Photo History of
TANKS
in Two World Wars

George Forty

BLANDFORD PRESS

POOLE · DORSET

First Published in the UK 1984 by Blandford Press Ltd,
Link House, West Street, Poole, Dorset, BH15 1LL

Copyright © 1984 Blandford Press Ltd.
Distributed in the United States by
Sterling Publishing Co., Inc.,
2 Park Avenue, New York, NY 10016
ISBN 07137 1216 3

British Library Cataloguing in Publication Data

Forty, George
  A photo history of tanks in two world wars.
  1. Tanks (Military science)—History—Pictorial
  works
  I. Title
  623.74'75'0222   UG446.5

Filmset by Keyspools Ltd, Golborne, Lancashire, U.K.
Printed in the U.K. by BAS Printers Ltd

Half-title page: British Heavy Tank Mark IV Female in France
during World War 1.

Frontispiece: Pershings of the American 2nd Armored Division
pass the shell-torn town hall in Magdeburg, Germany, after
clearing the city on 18 April 1945.

Contents

S 7068495

Churchill AVRE. A graphic picture taken on the Normandy beaches on 6 June 1944, showing medics treating a casualty under the shelter of the comforting armoured side of a Churchill AVRE. The Armoured Vehicle Royal Engineers, was a perfect AFV for Sapper's use, being roomy enough inside to carry plenty of engineer's stores, while providing excellent protection for the assault engineers. The main gun was replaced by a type of spigot mortar, which fire a 40 lb bomb (known as the Flying Dustbin) some 80 yds. It was ideal for demolishing concrete obstacles. This AVRE would have been in the 1st Assault Brigade, Royal Engineers, of 79th Armoured Division.

Introduction

This book is not intended to be either a dictionary of tanks, or an encyclopaedia. It is rather a photographic evocation of tank design over its first thirty years, namely from 1915 to 1945. It covers the evolution of the tank, its initial hesitant use during World War 1, its development in the 1920s and 1930s, and finally its rise to power during World War 2, when it became the major decision maker in land warfare.

I have deliberately tried to show as many different models of tanks as possible, although concentrating on those which actually saw active service. I have also contrasted the differing styles of tank design between the various major tank producing countries, but at the same time showing that other, smaller producers were still able to make their important contributions to the overall story of armoured development. In order to show the versatility of the tank and tank designer, I have deliberately included some of the many derivatives of the basic tank, such as tank destroyers, self-propelled guns, armoured engineer and recovery vehicles, plus examples of the host of specialised armour. It is also interesting to note that, despite the fact that tank design was only in its infancy in World War 1, specialised armour was still considered necessary, so the bridge-layer, mine clearing vehicle, amphibians and the like, were not merely inventions of World War 2 tank designers.

All the photographs in this book come from a remarkable collection owned by the well known graphic artist, John Batchelor. They form but a small part of his immense photo library and I am extremely indebted to him for their use. I am also indebted to the Tank Museum Library for allowing me access to the necessary sources of material from which to prepare the captions.

George Forty

Bryantspuddle.
July 1983

7

1 Evolution

From the earliest times man has searched for better and more powerful weapons with which to defend himself, or to attack and destroy his enemies. As each new weapon appeared on the battlefield it must have seemed all powerful to those engaged in combat – the club, the bow and arrow, the chariot, the knight in full armour, the first firearm – the list is well known, culminating today in what must surely be the ultimate weapons of mass destruction, the nuclear, chemical and biological horrors with which we threaten the very existence of the human race.

However, no weapon system has had more impact on the actual battlefield as the tank. It was a revolutionary weapon system, combining the three basic essentials of firepower, protection and mobility. These characteristics can be applied to every armoured fighting vehicle (AFV) which appears in this book. Firepower is the most important; after all, it is the *raison d'être* of the tank, to carry about on the battlefield guns and crews to serve them with the minimum interference from the enemy. Protection and mobility must be balanced one against the other, because it is clear that the larger and heavier the tank, then the more powerful the engine and transmission systems must be, or the slower and more easily engaged will be the resulting AFV. By applying this balance in differing ways, designs can range from the lightly armoured scout tank, relying on speed and agility for its protection, to the great lumbering monsters, whose thick armour makes them impervious to all but the heaviest enemy fire, always provided they can reach the right place at the right time to do their job!

The tank came into existence because of a number of factors, such as the ability to produce, machine and rivet armour plate; the invention of the complicated machinery necessary to carry out heavy engineering; the advent of the internal combustion engine and the availability of fuel to run it. However, above all, it was the vision and determination of a small band of dedicated pioneers, mainly British, although to be fair, the French were only a step behind. These men went on, despite many setbacks, to produce their revolutionary new ideas and to see them to fruition. They had to fight against a great deal of prejudice, which continued within the British Army long after World War 1, and led to Britain being ill-prepared for World War 2. They were helped immeasurably by an equally small number of far-sighted politicians, the foremost being Winston Churchill, who, in spite of lack of funds and lack of interest by the majority of the Army, managed to keep the 'Landships' project alive by interesting the Navy in it. Not without good reason were the first tanks known by the initials 'HMLS' – His Majesty's Land Ships.

I have deliberately confined the photographs in this part of the book to actual tanks, that is to say, track laying armoured vehicles, driven under their own power by an engine. The only reason for ignoring the steps that went before the building of the No 1 *Lincoln Machine* is one of restricted space. Clearly there were track laying vehicles, albeit unarmoured ones, running some years before *Little Willie*, while the wheeled armoured car had already proved its effectiveness before tanks ever came on the scene.

Heavy Tank Mark I. The building of the first batch of 100 Mark I tanks began in February 1916, following the same basic design as *Mother*. They were called 'tanks' for security reasons, to disguise their true purpose. Although there were some minor variations in later models, this outline shape remained fairly constant, as it was found to have an excellent cross country performance. Half of the first batch were to be Male tanks with 6-pdr guns, the rest Female with two machine guns in each sponson. It was not until after the first tank *versus* tank engagement (in April 1918) that the danger of having a tank with no effective weapon capable of penetrating an enemy tank was realised and thereafter hermaphrodite tanks with one 6-pdr sponson and one dual machine gun sponson were introduced. The Mark I is recognisable by its tail wheels and the anti-grenade and bomb roof (usually covered with chicken wire which is missing in this photograph). The Mark I had a crew of eight men, four of whom had to work together in order to change direction! The other four manned the sponson armament.

I EVOLUTION

The First Tank

Chariots of Iron. 'And the Lord was with Judah; and he drove out the inhabitants of the mountain; but he could not drive out the inhabitants of the valley, because they had chariots of iron.' (Judges Chapter 1, Verses 19 & 20.) Probably the earliest ancestor of the tank was the war chariot, like those mentioned in this quotation from the Holy Bible, or the one shown in this drawing from the ancient city of Ur of the Chaldees which dates from about the year 3500 BC.

The No 1 *Lincoln Machine*. Designed by William Tritton (later Sir), chief executive of William Foster & Co Ltd of Lincoln and Lt W. G. Wilson, then an RNAS armoured car officer, the 'Tritton Machine', as it was sometimes called, was designed and constructed between 2 August and 8 September 1915. It weighed about 18 tons. Above its rectangular hull was to have been a centrally mounted turret with a 2-pdr gun. However, this was not fitted and a dummy turret of the correct weight was used when the machine was tested. The machine had Bullock tracks, brought from America, where they had been developed commercially from an original British design. Tail wheels helped the cross-country performance and aided steering. It suffered from track problems, through lack of grip and an inclination for the tracks to come off when crossing trenches. Speed was between $\frac{3}{4}$ and 2 mph. It could just about cross a 4 ft wide trench and mount a 2 ft vertical step.

Little Willie. In order to meet the War Office revised requirements, to cross a 5 ft trench and climb a 4½ ft step, the No 1 *Lincoln Machine* was rebuilt, using the original hull and engine (6-cylinder Daimler petrol engine, developing 105 bhp at 100 rpm), but with completely redesigned tracks replacing the Bullock tracks. The track frames were increased in length to improve cross country performance. The simulated turret was also removed and *Little Willie* was completed early in December 1915. (Presumably the name had some ribald connection with the Kaiser.) The new tracks comprised cast steel plates rivetted to links which had guides engaging with rails on the side of the track frames. This pattern of track construction was used for all British tanks up to 1918.

Little Willie. Seen here on test at Lincoln on 3 December 1915, with the new Tritton tracks weighted down with cast iron slabs, *Little Willie* is still preserved at the Tank Museum, Bovington Camp.

William Foster & Co. Ltd. A general view inside one of the tank construction sheds at William Foster & Co. Ltd of Lincoln. Note the simple basic design of the early tanks. The Daimler engines are seen in the centre, between two rows of tank hulls. Fosters continued to be the major producers of tanks throughout World War I.

Mother. Even while *Little Willie* was being built, Tritton and Wilson were working on a new design, which had a much longer track length in order to improve its cross country performance and to be sure of meeting the new War Office requirements – to cross a 5 ft trench and climb a $4\frac{1}{2}$ ft step. It had been worked out that this could be achieved by a wheel 60 ft in diameter, so the length of the track on the ground and its shape had to be the same as the lower curve of a wheel that size. This meant raising the height of the front horns and gave rise to the now familiar rhomboidal shape common to all of the British World War I heavy tanks. In order to keep the centre of gravity low it was decided to mount the tank's main armament – two naval 6-pdr guns – in side sponsons. During her life *Mother* had various names such as *Big Willie* and *Centipede*, but as the very first battle tank she was rightly called *Mother* – despite her Male armament (as later photographs show, Female tanks had machine guns instead of 6-pdrs). Weighing 28 tons, with a top speed of nearly 4 mph, *Mother* first moved under her own power on 21 August 1915. Sadly, she was reduced to scrap at the start of World War 2. *Mother* is seen here on test at Burton Park, Lincoln.

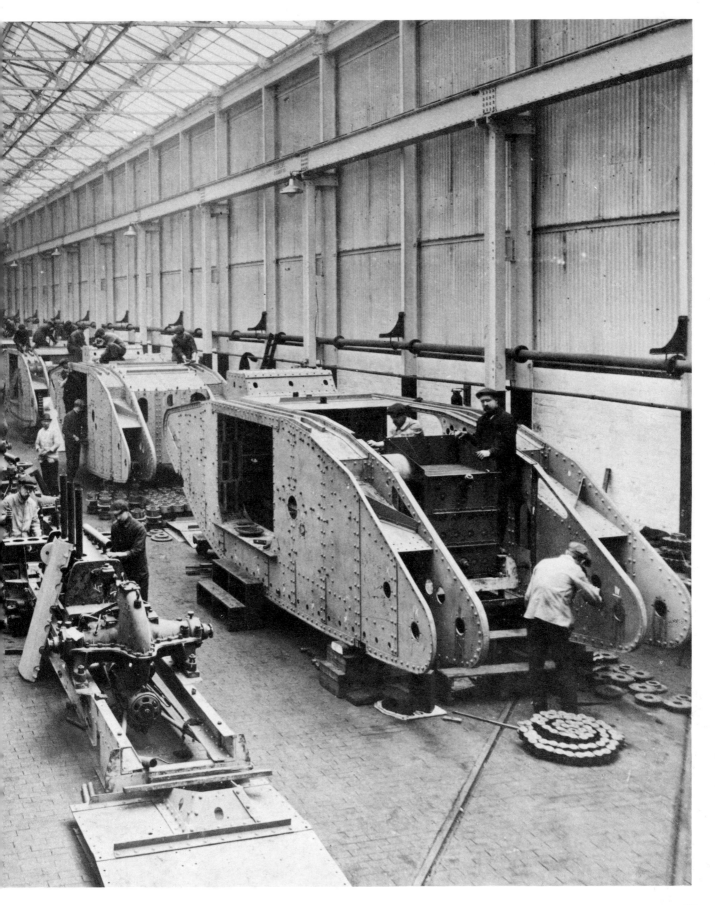

2 The Great War

Almost from its outset, World War I developed certain characteristics which set it apart from other wars. Foremost of these was the horrendous casualty figures which became commonplace after almost every battle. The machine gun and the artillery shell first decimated, then all but annihilated, the cream of the youth of Europe. Next was the appearance of the battlefield. The power of modern explosives, the heavy equipment, the thousands of feet, hooves and wheels combined with the elements of wind, rain, snow and sleet, rapidly turned the landscape into a featureless mass of churned up mud and water, making progress difficult if not downright impossible. The third main characteristic was the digging. To escape the shell and the bullet, the soldiers dug into the ground, first simple trenches, then more elaborate positions, protected by miles of barbed wire, thousands of trip flares and a wide variety of mines, to kill and maim the enemy. The opposing forces each created their own labyrinth of underground shelters, but most typical were the opposing snake-like lines of narrow trenches, in which the fighting soldiers eked out a precarious existence. 'If you knows a better 'ole, go to it' remarks Bruce Bairnsfather's immortal 'Old Bill' taciturnly to his mate, as they wait, Short Lee Enfield rifles at the ready, to give the Boche 'what for'. The only 'better 'ole' they would see would be, in all probability, the grave.

Introduce into this situation a revolutionary new weapon system, one that could get across the broken, shell-torn ground, over the lines of trenches, easily surmounting their high parapets, carrying with it guns and men, protected from the dreaded machine guns and shell splinters. Here then was the solution to breaking the everlasting stalemate without the dreadful 'butcher's bill' which everyone had come to expect. Naturally this dream did not come true overnight. World War I witnessed the introduction and improvement of various types of AFVs – first armoured cars, then heavy tanks, light tanks, gun carriers and then the whole gamut of specialised armoured vehicles, the need for which became apparent as armoured warfare became more sophisticated. So the first bridgelayers, command vehicles, bulldozers, mine exploders and all the rest made their appearance. By the end of the war, the tank had shown itself to be a battle-winning factor, provided it was used properly, in sufficient numbers and over reasonable going. Its devastating shock action had been proved conclusively by the British at the Battle of Cambrai in November 1917, but it would be left to another generation of their erstwhile opponents to prove how really effective the armoured fighting vehicle could be when properly handled as part of an all arms team.

In this portion of the book I have illustrated the main tanks which fought on both sides, concentrating on the nations who were most concerned, namely Britain and France. By late 1918, both numbered their tank forces in thousands, the British heavies and the French lights being pre-eminent. The Germans, although they recognised the potential of the new weapon system, never exploited it properly, their total tank production, discounting prototypes, being under twenty, although they did make good use of a fair number of captured enemy tanks as the photographs show. On 2 October 1918, General Ludendorff, while reporting to the German Parliament, said: '... there is no longer any prospect or possibility of compelling the enemy to peace. Above all two facts have been decisive for this issue: first, the tanks ...'

'The First Tank Attack.' 'A tank is walking up the High Street of Flers with the British Army cheering behind' – so read the headlines in the British Press on 16 September 1916, heralding the first use of the new weapon the previous day in an attempt to bolster up the Somme offensive begun nearly three months earlier. There had been over 60,000 British casualties on the very first day of the attack and it was hoped that the tanks would be able to break the stalemate of trench warfare. Unfortunately, on this and other occasions until the battle of Cambrai in November 1917, tanks were used spread out in 'penny packets', rather than concentrated, thus wasting much of their effectiveness. (Note that the photograph does not actually show the Flers engagement; and that the tank is a later model, a Mark II Male.)

2 THE GREAT WAR

British Heavy Tanks

Heavy Tank Mark II Male (*Below*) **and Female** (*Bottom*). In all some 150 Mark I heavy tanks were produced and delivered to the Army. As a result of their impact upon the battlefield, the Commander-in-Chief, Field Marshal Sir Douglas Haig, ordered a further 1000 tanks to be built. First of these were 50 Mark IIs – 25 Male and 25 Female. They were almost identical to the Mark I, apart from minor alterations resulting from the limited battle experience of the Mark Is on the Somme. The tail wheels were discar-ded, there was a revised hatch on top, and a wider track shoe at every sixth track link in order to improve traction. Armour on these early tanks had to be cut and drilled as soft steel and then hardened to inhibit hostile fire. The front plates were 10 mm thick, the sides 8 mm. The tank was built by rivetting sheets of armour plate to butt straps and angle iron. Inevitably, there were gaps, which allowed molten metal to penetrate inside when a joint was hit by small arms fire. This 'splash', as it was called, meant that the crew had to wear small steel masks with a chain mail visor hanging down over the face, to reduce injury. However, they were uncomfortable to wear and made it much more difficult to observe. The Mark II was 26 ft 5 ins long, 13 ft 9 ins wide and 8 ft high. The Mark III heavy tank was virtually identical to the Mark II except that it had slightly thicker armour. Fifty Mark IIIs (half Male and half Female) were built. The later Males were armed with the short barrelled 6-pdr gun, because naval guns proved too long for land use, banging into trees or becoming buried in the mud! Guns could fire either HE or AP shot.

Heavy Tank Mark IV Female (*Below*) **and Male** (*Bottom*). Designed in October 1916, the Mark IV was put into production in March/April 1917. More Mark IVs were built than any other model – a total of 1,220, of which 205 were tank tenders, with specially boosted 125 bhp Daimler engines. They were fitted with square box-like sponsons and used to carry tank supplies into battle. The Mark IV had various improvements, including an armoured 60-gallon petrol tank mounted outside the tank be- tween the rear horns. This was much safer than the earlier internal tanks, located on either side of the driver. Sponsons were hinged so that they could be swung inside during rail journeys, instead of having to be removed and carried separately. The size of the sponsons was reduced so that the bottoms were not so close to the ground. In both versions, the Vickers and Hotchkiss machine guns were replaced by Lewis guns, but these proved a great disappointment and later had to be replaced with modified Hotchkiss machine guns. Thicker steel was used in the construction of the Mark IV, 12 mm in front and on the sides, decreasing to 8 mm elsewhere. This made it proof against the German anti-tank rifle. The first Mark IVs went into action on 7 June 1917 at the Battle of Messines Ridge. The Male tank 2341 bears a 'Chinese Eye' on its sides, as it was paid for by Mr Eu Tong Sen of the Malay States.

Experimental unditching gear (*Above*). One of the best innovations was the provision of a beam of wood, reinforced with metal and weighing about $\frac{1}{2}$ ton, which was carried on top of the tank (see previous page, upper photograph). This was the unditching beam and could be attached by lengths of chain to the top run of the track. As the tracks revolved they pulled the beam under the belly of the tank, thus helping the tracks to gain sufficient purchase to get out of soft mud. This photograph shows an experimental unditching gear designed to prevent the crew having to expose themselves while fixing the unditching beam chains. Instead, the beam was permanently attached to two chains which passed all round the tank and could be connected to a main sprocket by means of an internal dog clutch. Although this idea worked on trials, it was never adopted.

The Tadpole Tail (*Centre left*). This was a device that could be fitted to either Mark IV or Mark V tanks, lengthening them by about 9 ft. The aim was to improve trench crossing capability, as the photograph illustrates. A further 28 track plates were needed on each track.

Mark IV with Stokes trench mortar (*Bottom left*). This Mark IV with a tadpole tail also incorporates an externally mounted Stokes trench mortar, which was invented in 1914 by Sir Wilfred Stokes and was the forerunner of the more familiar form of modern mortar, being a simple tube supported by a bipod.

Heavy Tank Mark V (*Right*). The major step forward achieved with the Mark V, designed in August 1917 and in the hands of troops in May 1918, was that one man could drive the tank by himself. This was because it was fitted with a four-speed epicyclic gearbox, designed by W. G. Wilson, epicyclic gearing and brakes replacing the change-speed gearing of earlier models. The engine was a purpose built Ricardo, developing 150 bhp at 1,250 rpm. The tank also had better observation and ventilation, while the 90 gallons of petrol contained in armour fuel tanks at the tail gave a radius of action of 45 miles compared with 24 of the early Marks and 35 of the Mark IV. 200 Males and 200 Females were built between December 1917 and June 1918.

Mark V with flexible tracks (*Below*). One experimental version of the Mark V was fitted with 'Snake' flexible tracks which were being tested for Medium D project (see later). These tests took place after the Armistice. A great success, it reached nearly 20 mph – normal top speed was $4\frac{1}{2}$ mph! – but it had been lightened considerably by removing sponsons and other gear.

Heavy Tank Mark V★. Although the Tadpole Tail (see earlier) had improved trench crossing ability, it lacked both rigidity and lateral stability. The most ideal solution came with the Mark V★, when an additional 6 ft of armour was added between the sponson opening and the epicyclic gear housing. Not only did this prove to be a most satisfactory construction, it also allowed additional storage space to carry up to 25 men or the equivalent weight of stores. About 600 were built and saw continual operational use, which proved their value. The weight went up from 29 to 33 tons and, because the engine power was not increased, the tank was much less manoeuvrable and slower than the Mark V.

Heavy Tank Mark V★★. This Mark had a more powerful Ricardo engine, producing 225 bhp at 1,250 rpm, which was mounted further back so that the commander's turret could be brought up nearer the front of the tank. The basic shape of the tank was different, allowing for another 6 ft of track to be in contact with the ground, giving improved steering. Although 300 were ordered, only 25 were ever built, before it was superseded by orders for the Mark VIII and Mark IX.

Heavy Tank Mark V★★★. As seen here, this model was only built in mock-up form in 1918.

Heavy Tank Mark VI (*Left*). Another interesting design that never went further than the mock-up stage. As will be seen, there were to be no gun sponsons, but rather a single 6-pdr, in the front of the tank, mounted quite low down. Designed in 1917, there was some American interest shown in this model, but it waned when the Mark VIII was designed later that same year.

Support Tank Mark IX (*Right*). This 27-tonner can truly be described as the first ever armoured personnel carrier, as it could carry up to 30 fully equipped soldiers in addition to its crew of four. An alternative load was 10 tons of stores, with additional storage space available on the roof or in special sledges, which could be towed along behind the tank. Only 35 of the 200 Mark IXs ordered were ever built (in later 1918) and only twelve reached troops. Various marks of heavy tanks, not needed in battle, were actually used for carrying stores over the mud and appalling going, their normal sponsons being replaced by square box-shaped ones of mild steel. This happened to a good many Mark Is as the Mark IVs arrived in France to replace them, and also later to some Mark IVs (about 205 of them).

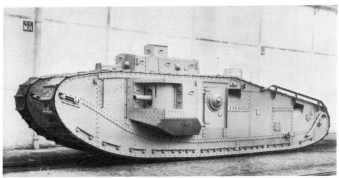

Heavy Tank Mark VII (*Above*). Although 75 Mark VIIs were originally ordered, only three were ever built and only one of these was completed before the Armistice. It was 3 ft longer than the Mark V and the 150 bhp Ricardo engine was coupled to two Williams Janney hydraulic gears, one to each track, through which power could be applied to either track in all speeds both in forward and reverse gears. This made the tank very manoeuverable and improved its cross country performance.

Heavy Tank Mark VIII (*Centre left*). Instead of just improving on existing Marks, the Mark VIII was an entirely new design. The 'International', as it was called, was the largest, heaviest and most powerful of all the British World War 1 heavy tanks. It had a Ricardo V-12 (or Liberty V-12) engine, producing 300 bhp at 1,250 rpm. At 37 tons it was a good 9 tons heavier than the Mark I, with a power to weight ratio about double. This was to have been a joint Anglo-American venture, to build in all some 4,450 tanks, 'to win the war in 1919', along with 2,000 Mark X, which never reached a full design stage. However, the Armistice rapidly put paid to these grandiose ideas and, although about 100 Mark VIIIs were built by the Americans after the war, only five were ever completed before the Armistice and only three of these reached the troops. With two 6-pdrs, seven machine guns, and a separate engine compartment (the first heavy tank to have one), it had great potential and would undoubtedly have been a battle winner.

Fascines and Cribs. In order to improve the obstacle crossing ability of heavy tanks, bundles of brushwood, known as fascines, were made up (10 ft long and $4\frac{1}{2}$ ft in diameter) bound with chains. The fascine was then mounted on the nose of the tank ready to be dropped into a deep trench for the tank to move across. They weighed $1\frac{1}{2}$ tons and were later replaced by hexagonal timber cribs (seen here) which were considerably lighter, but were used in exactly the same way.

Message away! I make no apology for including this famous photograph of a pigeon being released from a tank, as it emphasises far better than words how difficult communications must have been before the advent of wireless. Later, heavy tanks did have semaphore arms on top, for signalling, but there were no real external – or internal – communications until wireless was fitted.

Wireless Tank. During a visit to the Tank Corps Central Workshops at Erin in France, Her Majesty Queen Mary is shown a wireless tank, a converted Female with some of its guns removed. Leaning against the tank is General Sir Hugh Elles, commander of the Tank Corps.

A Tank Bridge. These three photographs show how the 20 ft tank bridge, carried by the Mark V** Engineer tank, was launched. The bridge was carried slung from a jib at the front of the tank (*left*). The jib was hinged, so that it could be raised and lowered, thus raising or lowering the bridge for positioning (*below left*). Having laid the bridge, the jib could then be detached, and if necessary the tank could now move across the bridge (*below right*).

Anti-Mine Rollers. These two photographs show two different types of anti-mine rollers, designed to set off enemy anti-tank mines at a safe distance in front of the tank.

An unditching beam in use. The beam is about to pass under the tank and will provide a purchase to enable the tank to extricate itself.

6-pdr gun. A good internal view of a 6-pdr gun in its cradle on the left-hand side of a Mark VIII heavy tank.

Gun Carrier Mark I. The appalling cross country going of the shell-torn battlefields made it impossible on many occasions to get field artillery up to support the infantry, leaving them very vulnerable to enemy counter attacks. To overcome this, the gun-carrying tank was designed. It could carry forward the 60-pdr or 6 in howitzer. It was possible to fire the howitzer from the carrier but the 60-pdr had to be dismounted first. A 105 bhp Daimler engine was mounted at the rear of the box-like body and the vehicle was driven from the strange driver's and brakesman's turrets on either side of the gun cradle. Forty-eight gun carriers were ordered in late 1916 and reached France in July 1917 in time to be used during the Third Battle of Ypres.

A dummy heavy tank is moved up to the front by real horse power!

Gun Carrier Mark I. When not carrying guns, the gun carriers could instead carry a great deal of ammunition, a typical load being 200 6 in shells, weighing about 10 tons. During the Third Battle of Ypres, they carried forward several hundreds of tons of ammunition.

British Medium Tanks

The Prototype Medium A, Whippet (*Top right*). Although the heavy tank was ideal to support infantry and to smash its way through the enemy positions, it was very slow and cumbersome, being unable to move at more than walking pace. There was, therefore, a need for a lighter, faster tank to supplement the cavalry and exploit the successes of the heavy tanks. Sir William Tritton was the designer of a high speed, lightly armoured tank in 1915, called the *Tritton Chaser* and christened *Whippet*, which became the tank's name. The prototype Medium A, which had an unarmoured, rounded fuel tank at the rear is shown.

Tank Medium A, Whippet (*Above*). An excellent shot of *Julian's Baby*, a Medium A, near the front in France. It is a typical production model, built by Foster's of Lincoln from December 1917, the total number of Whippets built being 200. It weighed 14 tons, had a crew of three and was armed with three Hotchkiss machine guns.

Tank Medium B, Whippet (*Top right*). As can be seen, the shape of the Medium B was more like that of the heavy tank than its predecessor, but with a large fixed turret mounted on top at the front of the hull. The Medium B weighed 18 tons and was longer and wider than the Medium A, but not so tall. The engine, a 4-cylinder 100 bhp Ricardo, was mounted in a separate compartment, with a bulkhead to divide it from the crew of four – the first tank ever to have this feature. A total of 48 Medium Bs were built, but none were ever used in action.

Tank Medium C (*Centre right*). Although it was designed in late 1917, none of the 45 Medium Cs built actually left the factory until after the Armistice. They remained in service until 1925, and proved to be a remarkably effective tank, with a better performance than any of the previous Mediums. At 20 tons, its 150 bhp Ricardo engine, gave it a power to weight ratio of 7.5 while its fuel tanks held 150 gallons – over double that of the Medium A. Top speed was still only 8 mph, but its radius of action was 120 miles.

Tank Medium D (*Bottom right*). The very last tank to be designed in World War 1 was the Medium D, seen here in wooden mock-up – it never got further than this design stage. However, sometime after the war, various modified models were produced and the Johnson Light Infantry Tank was based on the Medium D design.

Tank Medium A with Modified tracks (*Left*). The Medium A was powered by two 45 hp Tyler lorry engines, set side by side in the front of the tank. Each had its own clutch and constant mesh four-speed gearbox, and each drove one track through a bevel box and cross shaft. The Whippet had a top speed in excess of 8 mph and a radius of action of 80 miles. Various attempts were made to improve the speed. The photograph shows a Medium A with a larger engine and sprung tracks (the Whippet was unsprung) evolved by Col. Philip Johnson, which could reach speeds of over 20 mph. The engine was a Rolls-Royce aeroplane engine.

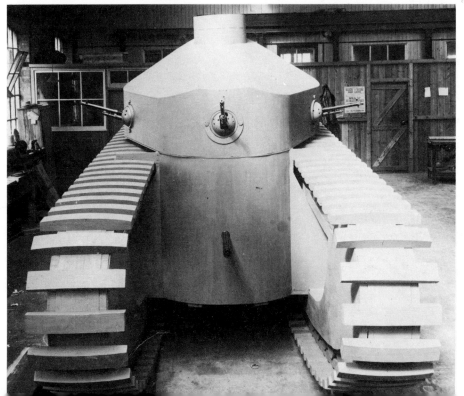

French Heavy Tanks

Schneider CA1. This was the first French tank to be designed. It was based upon the Holt tractor. The first of the 400 built was delivered in September 1916, so they were not far behind the British. The driving force was a Colonel (later General) Jean Baptiste Estienne, who is reputed to have said: 'Whoever shall first be able to make land ironclads armed and equipped ... will have won the war.' Designed by Eugene Brille of the Schneider Company, the Char d'Assault Schneider 1, to give its full title, weighed $13\frac{1}{2}$ tons, mounted a 75 mm gun in a sponson on the righthand side of the tank and two 8 mm machine guns. It had a crew of seven men.

Schneider CA1 (*Left*). This photograph shows the other side of the Schneider, a late production model, with the main access door open at the rear. It had better protected fuel tanks and more roof ventilation than earlier models. The Schneider was powered by a 55 hp engine, giving the tank a top speed of $4\frac{1}{2}$ mph and a radius of action of 30 miles.

Saint Chamond (*Left and Below*). The other French heavy tank, the Saint Chamond, was designed by a Colonel Rimailho and built in 1916 by the Compagnie des Forges et Aciéries de la Marine et d'Homércourt, whose factory at Saint Chamond gave the tank its name. At 23 tons, it was heavier than the Schneider, had a crew of nine and mounted a 75 mm gun on its nose, and had four machine guns. The photograph at left shows one moving into action, complete with mascot! A total of 400 was built and the tank first saw action in early May 1917. Its cross country performance was indifferent, as it tended to bury its nose when negotiating soft going. It had an electric transmission, a 90 hp Panhard motor driving a dynamo which powered two electric motors – one per track. Seen below is the improved model, the two cylindrical cupolas having been replaced by a pitched roof. Late models still had a single, flat topped cupola on the right for the driver. The original gun has been replaced by the regular 75 mm Model 1897 field gun. Top speed was 5.3 mph.

French Light Tanks

Renault FT17 (*Right*). Designed by Louis Renault, with the support of the irrepressible Gen. Estienne, the Char Mitrailleuse Renault FT17, was a remarkable little tank, a true milestone in design which lasted right up to the start of World War 2, and was adapted and produced by many countries all over the world. The American Ford 6-ton tank, for example, was in essence an American built Renault FT. A very large number of FT17s were built, of seven different models, the one seen here having a moulded turret. One unique aspect of the tank was its fully revolving turret – the first tank in the world to have all-round traverse. Armed with an 8 mm Hotchkiss machine gun, the two man tank weighed 6½ tons and was powered by a 35 hp Renault engine.

FT17 in American Service (*Bottom right*). This FT17 belongs to the French Tank Force – Artillerie Speciale. However, a number of similar light tanks were used by the US Army to equip the 344th and 345th Light Tank Battalions. They first saw action on 12 September 1918, under command of Lt Col. George S. Patton Jr, in an attack against the St Mihiel Salient. The photograph shows clearly the hinged access doors, with the driver seated immediately behind them. The gunner's position was in the centre of the tank, directly under the turret.

Char-canon FT17 (*Below*). The two FTs nearest the camera are armed with the 37 mm Puteaux gun, in an angled, rivetted turret. Over 1,800 FT17s were armed with the 37 mm gun, mounted in both rivetted or cast turrets.

FT17 in British Service (*Left*). The British also made good use of the little FT17, although mainly in the liaison or command roles. When this was done the gun was taken out – as seen here. I wonder what the General is asking the young lance corporal, whilst the tank driver stands beside his vehicle.

Fascine tank (*Below left*). The French used fascines for obstacle crossing just as the British did, carrying them in a cradle on the front of the tank. The fascines could be dropped into the wide trenches using a release mechanism operated from inside the tank, so that no-one was exposed to the enemy.

Char-canon Renault BS (*Above*). The largest gun mounted in an FT17 was a short barrelled 75 mm gun, in a seven-sided turret. It put the tank's weight up to 7.2 tons. Not one of the BS (Batterie de Support) version was completed before the Armistice, although the few that were built later were used in between the wars in North Africa. They were still in service ready to engage the Allied *Torch* landing forces in 1942, operated by the Vichy French.

Bulldozer tank (*Left*). A bulldozer version of the FT17 had the turret and driver's hatches removed and replaced by a roof of sheet metal. Note the windows in the blade so that the driver could see where he was going!

31

Bridgelayer tank (*Above*). This was very possibly the earliest tank bridgelayer in the world. The one-piece bridge was pushed forward over the obstacle to be crossed. It was never used in combat.

Searchlight tank (*Right*). After the war, the French police adapted the FT17 for use during internal security operations. A tall mast was mounted on the tank, which carried two searchlights on the top. These could be turned 360° or pointed downwards in any direction.

Amphibious tank (*Below right*). There was even an amphibious model of the FT17, seen here entering the River Seine, close to the Renault factory. It worked quite well in the water (*inset*).

SP gun version (*Above*). In 1918, trials were held with a modified FT chassis, on which had been mounted a long barrelled 105 mm gun. The trials went quite well, but the project was abandoned in November 1918.

Command tank. The Char Renault TSF (Telegraph Sans Fil – wireless) Command tank), was widely used, the normal turret being replaced by a box-like structure. One of these Signal tanks can be seen at the rear of this column of FT17s.

Dummy tank. There was even a wooden FT17 dummy!

American Tanks

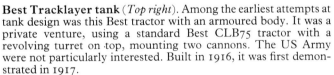

Best Tracklayer tank (*Top right*). Among the earliest attempts at tank design was this Best tractor with an armoured body. It was a private venture, using a standard Best CLB75 tractor with a revolving turret on top, mounting two cannons. The US Army were not particularly interested. Built in 1916, it was first demonstrated in 1917.

Holt HA36 tank (*Right*). This small, one-man tank, was built by the Holt Tractor Company in 1916. It was powered by a small engine and had wooden guns. In basic shape it resembled the British heavy tanks.

Holt G9 tank (*Above*). Another early tank to be built by the Holt Tractor Company was the G9, which was based upon a 75 bhp, 10-ton tractor, armoured and with a small turret on top at the front and a larger one at the rear. It was tested in 1917 but not adopted.

Holt Gas-Electric tank. One of the first American tanks to be built was the Holt Gas-Electric which, like the French St Chamond, was a petrol-electric tank. A Holt 90 bhp petrol engine produced the power to a generator which then ran two electric motors, one for each track. Main armament was a 75 mm howitzer, mounted in the nose (but obscured by the soldier in this photograph).

Skeleton tank (*Right*). This weird looking device was built by the Pioneer Tractor Company of Winona, Minnesota. In order to keep its weight down (it only weighed 9 tons) the tank was built in skeleton form, using ordinary iron piping, with an armoured boxlike compartment for the two man crew at its heart. It had a good cross country performance due to its light weight – its length and width were similar to that of the 28-ton British heavy tank. The skeleton tank did not get further than the prototype stage.

Steam tank (*Right*). The US Engineer Corps produced the Steam tank in 1918, using the layout and characteristics of the British heavy tank, although it was much heavier, 50 tons. Armament comprised a newly invented flamethrower and four machine guns. Propulsion was by two steam engines, each with its own boiler and driving one track. A speed of 4 mph was achieved, but, although the tank was shipped over to France for trials in 1918, it did not arrive there until the war had ended, so was never used.

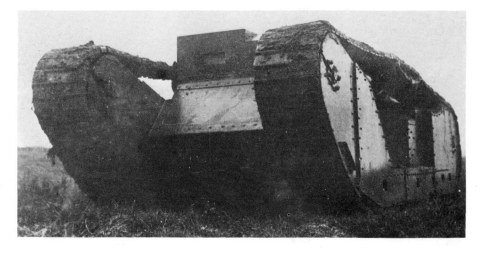

Studebaker tank (*Right*). Built by the Studebaker Pierce-Arrow Export Corporation, following an order from the British War Mission in USA in 1917. Like all the rest of the American designed tanks of World War 1, apart from the Ford 3-ton and six-ton (see the next page), it did not get further than the prototype stage.

Ford 3-ton tank. The US Army tank battalions which saw action in France were equipped either with British heavy tanks or French light tanks. In 1918, Ford built a two-man tank, using the same characteristics and basic design of the highly successful French Renault FT17. It was the cheapest and smallest tank built in the USA and undoubtedly the most successful. Driver and gunner both sat at the front. The tank was powered by two Model T Ford engines, producing 40 bhp between them. The prototype was sent to France and arrived in time to be tested and approved before the Armistice. Although over 15,000 were originally ordered, only fifteen were ever built.

The Liberty tank. Although we have already covered this tank in the British section, it must also appear here because the Americans built far more of the Mark VIII Liberty tank (also called the International) than Britain did. In all, 100 Mark VIIIs were completed at the Rock Island Arsenal in 1919–20. Withdrawn from service in 1932, they were stored until 1939 when, on the outbreak of war, many were sent to Canada for use as training vehicles.

Six-ton tank M1917. Copied directly from the French Renault FT tank, the M1917 was known initially as the Six-ton Special Tractor for security reasons. Although nearly 1,000 of these tanks were built, only 64 had been finished before the end of the war and of these only ten reached France. There were numerous improvements over the French design including replacing the steel-rimmed wooden idler wheels on the Renault with all-steel ones; fitting a self-starter to the 4-cylinder Buda engine; constructing a bulkhead between the crew and the engine compartment. They continued in service for many years, and like the Liberty tank, were given to Canada for training purposes in 1939. The USA supplied a total of 300 tanks to Canada at the start of World War 2.

2 THE GREAT WAR
German and Italian Tanks

A7V Sturmpanzerwagen prototype. At the start of World War 1 there were a number of proposals put forward for various types of tank projects. However, the Germans lacked anyone at Minister level prepared to really put his weight behind any project. Consequently, no serious attempt was made to build one until after the early British tanks had appeared on the battlefield, and even then there was little enthusiasm. Only one German tank type took part in battle, the A7V, 100 being ordered but less than twenty built.

A7Vs in action. A pair of German tanks near Villers-Cotterels in 1918. The first tank *versus* tank battle took place at Villers-Bretonneux on 24 April 1918 when three British tanks, two Female and one Male, met three A7Vs supporting some German infantry. Two of the enemy were too far away to engage, but the British Male, a Mark IV, soon opened up on the leading A7V. The crews of the British tanks had been badly gassed the previous day. Two of the Mark IV Male's crew had been evacuated and the rest were suffering from the effects of the mustard gas, their eyes puffed up and smarting burns on exposed skin. Consequently, it was difficult to see properly to engage the enemy. Their first rounds missed and the A7V quickly replied with armour piercing machine gun fire, causing 'splash' and sparks inside the British tank. The enemy engaged the two Female tanks, damaging both and forcing them to withdraw. The British commander of the Male, Second Lt Frank Mitchell, halted his tank to give his gunner a steady shot. They were both delighted to see the enemy heel over, but it had simply run down a steep bank and overturned.

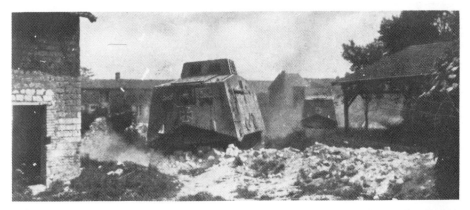

A7V Sturmpanzerwagen. Here, an A7V, captured in battle, arrives at the Tank Corps Central Workshops, Erin, France, for investigation. Weighing 30 tons, it had an enormous crew of eighteen, twelve of whom were machine gunners, divided into teams of two, and mounted a 57 mm gun in the nose and six machine guns. At $26\frac{1}{4}$ ft long, 10 ft wide and nearly 11 ft tall, it was about the same length as British heavy tanks, but narrower and taller. The A7V was powered by two 4-cylinder Daimler-Benz engines, mounted side by side and each producing 100 bhp. Cross country performance was poor, although its top speed on roads was 8 mph.

A trophy of war. Captured by the 26th Battalion, AIF, this A7V now sports a British lion, complete with crown. The lion has an A7V under its paw (obscured by the nearest of the group of victorious Australian officers). The A7V had 24 bogey wheels, suspended from a sprung shaft, giving its occupants a much more comfortable ride than the crews of the unsprung British heavies.

Captured British Mark IV tank. The cross-country performance of the A7V was so poor that German tank crews much preferred to use captured enemy tanks. After an overhaul, the Male tanks were often rearmed with the Russian 57 mm Sokol guns, as fitted to the A7V.

Captured British Whippet. One complete German tank company was equipped with captured Whippets. *Beuterpanzerwagen* (*beute* is literally 'booty', loot or plunder) were very popular.

Leichte Kampfwagen I. The German light tank LKI was designed by Joseph Vollmer, who worked on the A7V. He advocated the use of simple, light tanks in preference to large, heavy, expensive ones. LKI only reached prototype stage before the Armistice. It weighed nearly 7 tons, had a three man crew and was armed with one machine gun. An LKII was designed, mounting a 57 mm gun and weighing nearer 9 tons due to its thicker armour. It also did not get further than prototype stage. There was to be an LKIII, again designed by Vollmer, with a 20 mm cannon. Although the Germans had hoped to build large numbers of these three light tanks their 'Plan 1919' never came to fruition.

Fiat 2000 heavy tank. Although Italy was an early user of armoured cars, they did not show much interest in tank development. The only Italian tank to be built was the Fiat 2000, the prototype of which is seen here. Five were eventually built and stayed in service until the early 1930s. It was powered by a 240 bhp engine, weighed 40 tons and had a crew of ten. Seven machine guns were mounted around its boxlike superstructure (not fitted in this photograph).

39

3 Developments Between the Wars

As the euphoria that marked the end of hostilities in 1918 died away, so did the need for building vast fleets of heavily armoured tanks to sweep across the battlefields of Europe. 'Tanks is tanks and tanks is dear, there shall be no tanks this year.' That quaint little rhyme from the USA, aptly sums up the situation that existed during the 1920s and 1930s on both sides of the Atlantic. In Britain and America, there were plenty of pioneers, both in the design of new armoured fighting vehicles and in their tactical handling, but for the most part, their voices remained unheeded. It was a prime example of British genius going to waste, through indifference, jealousy and sheer incompetence. At the end of World War 1 Britain held a tremendous lead over every other country in the world, with the possible exception of France, not only in the field of tank design, but also in the tactical handling of these remarkable new weapons. Twenty years later, when World War 2 was almost upon them, the British were still arguing amongst themselves, trying to decide what type of tanks should be built and how they should be used. Other nations, who had started with virtually no experience whatsoever, had, despite their own difficulties, caught Britain up and passed her.

If things were bad in Britain they were even worse in America. Here, the Tank Corps had been disbanded after World War 1 and tanks had become an insignificant part of the Infantry arm who had not the slightest idea how to use their firepower and mobility properly. Brilliant designers, such as Walter J. Christie, were forced to take their wares elsewhere, his design, for example, becoming the basis of the Russian medium tank fleet that was to astound the world in later years. When mechanisation came, as it inevitably had to, the US Cavalry were forced into the subterfuge of calling its tanks 'Combat Cars', so as not to offend the infantry! It is not surprising that brilliant soldiers such as George S. Patton and Dwight D. Eisenhower left the Tank Corps in disgust, nor that the Americans had under 400 tanks in service at the start of World War 2.

This situation undoubtedly frustrated many soldiers on both sides of the Atlantic and was to have a disastrous effect upon the Allied cause in the early years of World War 2. However, it would be wrong to imagine that no progress of any kind was made between the wars. Many designs were produced, especially of the light variety – 'Tankettes' as they were popularly called – that made up for their lack of armoured protection and firepower, by being cheap and reasonably easy to produce. They did have the merit of being adequate training vehicles, despite lacking the sophistication that armoured warfare required, like a rapid means of communications on the move. Some British models such as the Carden-Loyd tankette and the Vickers 6-ton light tank were bought, copied and then produced under licence, all over the world, as the realisation of the latent power of the new weapon spread.

Of all the major tank producing nations of World War 1, France alone did not falter in its conviction that the tank was a battle winning weapon. Their production continued and like the British they sold their tanks all over the world, many Renault FT17s still being in service at the start of World War 2. However, they also produced some formidable medium and heavy tanks for their own forces, until, by 1939, they were probably the best equipped tank army in the world. Sadly, the ability of the French senior officers to appreciate how these new weapons should be used had not kept pace with the tank designers. Like the Americans, the French tanks were subjugated to the Infantry arm, spread in 'penny packets' and used in a totally uncoordinated manner. They would thus prove easy meat for their opponents in the tactics of 'Lightning War' that was to hit them in 1940. I will leave the rise of the German armour until later. However, their technique of *Blitzkrieg* owed much to those British pioneers who had struggled with *ad hoc* armoured forces in the 1920s and 1930s, hammering out so painfully and against all obstacles the new way that wars should be fought.

As the photographs show, other, smaller countries, became the designers and producers of many worthwhile and effective AFVs, a good example being Czechoslovakia. Czech tank interest evolved initially from imported designs, but these were improved, produced locally, then sold all over the world. Undoubtedly this was helped by the fact that the German tank designer, Vollmer, settled in Czechoslovakia in the 1920s, after spending a few years in Sweden. Firms such as Skoda and CKD became highly competitive in the tank exporting business in the mid-1930s.

This part of the book briefly tells the story of those inter-war years and the photographs show the profound effect the period had worldwide, on tank design.

An interesting photograph of a British heavy tank being used by German Government Forces against the Spartacists, during the revolution in Berlin 1919. The Spartacists were a far leftist group, named after the slave who had led the rebellion against the Romans. The capital was close to anarchy by Christmas Eve 1918, and by early January 1919 the Reds controlled the public utilities, transportation and the munitions factories. Admitting openly that they were Communists, the Spartacists called for revolution and by mid-morning on 6 January, 200,000 workers carrying weapons and red flags had taken to the streets. The Free Corps, however, marched in from outside the city, crushed the centres of Communist resistance and murdered all the Spartacist leaders. Clearly, the tank was a *Beuterpanzerwagen* from World War 1.

3 DEVELOPMENTS BETWEEN THE WARS

British

Morris-Martel two-man tankette (*Below*). The idea of a light tank, so well demonstrated by the French Renault series in World War 1, was revived by the British in the early 1920s. One officer in particular, Major (later Lt General) Sir Giffard Le Q. Martel, built various machines at his own expense and then demonstrated them to the War Office. As a result, a number of these tankettes were built by Morris – both one and two-man versions. This is the two-man model which was armed with a machine gun, weighed 2¾ tons and could travel at about 15 mph on roads.

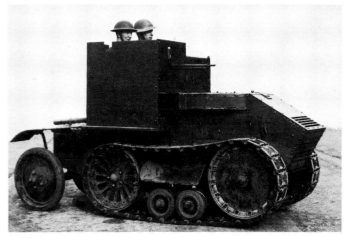

Amphibious Medium D (*Above left*). An early British attempt at an amphibious tank was this modified Medium D, known as the Medium D★★, which was used for water trials at Christchurch in 1921.

A1E1 Independent (*Centre left*). At the opposite end of the scale was this 31½-ton tank, multi-turreted and heavily armed, which was designed, as its name implies, for independent action. It was built in 1926, and in many respects its design was very advanced. It had a crew of eight who used laryngaphone communications. The controls were hydraulically operated and the steering was by wheel except for sharp turns. Main armament was a 3-pdr (47 mm) in the main turret, with four Vickers machine guns in subsidiary turrets. Its 398 bhp Armstrong Siddeley V-12 engine gave it a road speed of 25 mph.

Carrier Mark VI Carden-Loyd (*Bottom left*). Following on from the publicity which the trials of the Martel tankettes received, the firm of Carden-Loyd Tractors Ltd produced a series of cheap, light tracked vehicles. The Mark VI appeared in 1926, in the role of machine gun carrier. It carried a Vickers .303 or .50 machine gun, which could be dismounted. Various versions of this little 1½ ton carrier were exported all over the world and were subsequently built under licence. Later photographs in this part of the book include examples of such light tracked vehicles as the Italian CV33, Russian T27 and Polish TK3. It had a crew of two, and was powered by a Ford Model T engine.

Vickers light amphibious tank (*Top right*). In the early 1930s this highly successful little amphibious tank, weighing just over two tons, was developed by Vickers Armstrong. It was not adopted by the British Army, but was bought by many countries overseas, as later photographs will show. Its top speed was in excess of 25 mph on land, and it could travel at about $3\frac{1}{2}$ mph in the water.

Light tank Mark II (*Centre right*). Another model of the light tank series produced in the early 1930s was the Mark II, one of which was fitted with experimental flotation units on either side and an outboard motor at the rear. As will be seen it floated very well indeed, thanks to its close rivetted construction. It weighed about $4\frac{1}{4}$ tons.

Light tank Mark VI (*Below*). The first tank of the series with a two-man turret was the Mark V, built in 1935 and followed the next year by the Mark VI. The version in this photograph, the Mark VIB, was the most widely used of the British light tanks in World War 2, seeing action in France in 1940 and later in the Western Desert. It had a crew of three, weighed just over 5 tons, and was armed with a .50 and a .303 in machine gun. The vulnerability of these little AFVs, soon gave rise to their demise, their recce role being taken over by armoured cars.

Light tank Mark VIC (*Bottom right*). The very last of the series had its Vickers machine guns replaced by 7.92 mm and 15 mm Besa air-cooled machine guns. It also had wider suspension wheels and broader tracks. Here a patrol passes through a farmyard during aerodrome defence in the summer of 1941, 'somewhere in England'.

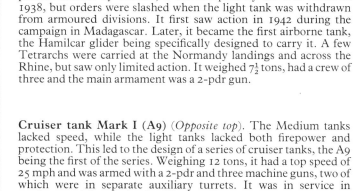

Light tank Mark VII (*Top left*). Known as the Tetrarch, this light tank had a very different design from its predecessors. Initially a private venture by Vickers, it was accepted by the War Office in 1938, but orders were slashed when the light tank was withdrawn from armoured divisions. It first saw action in 1942 during the campaign in Madagascar. Later, it became the first airborne tank, the Hamilcar glider being specifically designed to carry it. A few Tetrarchs were carried at the Normandy landings and across the Rhine, but saw only limited action. It weighed $7\frac{1}{2}$ tons, had a crew of three and the main armament was a 2-pdr gun.

Cruiser tank Mark I (A9) (*Opposite top*). The Medium tanks lacked speed, while the light tanks lacked both firepower and protection. This led to the design of a series of cruiser tanks, the A9 being the first of the series. Weighing 12 tons, it had a top speed of 25 mph and was armed with a 2-pdr and three machine guns, two of which were in separate auxiliary turrets. It was in service in 1938–41 and fought in the Western Desert. Although adequate against the Italian armour, it was no match for the contemporary German panzers. Another version mounted a 3.7 in howitzer for close-support.

Medium tank Mark I (*Centre left*). Following on from the Medium D, this Vickers-built $11\frac{3}{4}$-ton tank was originally called Light tank Mark I and production models came into service in 1924. It was later reclassified as Medium tank Mark I and was the first British tank with all-round traverse and geared elevation for the gun. Production of the Mark I and II amounted to some 160 tanks. The main armament was one 3-pdr (47 mm) QF gun, a 3.7 in howitzer being fitted in close-support tanks. Two Vickers machine guns were mounted in the hull sides, while there were four Hotchkiss machine guns carried in the turret for dismounted use. The crew was five (commander, driver, radio-operator and two gunners). It weighed nearly 12 tons. The 90 bhp Armstrong Siddeley V-8 engine gave it a top speed of 15–16 mph.

Medium tank Mark II★ (*Bottom left*). The Mark I was followed in 1925 by an improved model, the Mark II, which had thicker armour and skirting plates protecting its suspension. The Mark II★ also had co-axial Vickers machine gun, and a commander's cupola, while the Hotchkiss machine guns were no longer carried in the turret. Weighing $13\frac{1}{2}$ tons, it had a top speed of 15 mph on roads.

Medium Mark II Command tank (*Opposite bottom left*). The more mobile armoured forces became, the greater was the need for proper command and control that could move with the fighting tanks yet stay in touch with larger static headquarters. This command tank was developed in the early 1930s, with a dummy gun in a fixed turret, which contained two wireless sets. Apart from the obvious, large aerial on the side, the tank externally resembled a standard vehicle.

Infantry tank Mark I Matilda I (*Opposite bottom right*). Also called the A11, this small, but robust little tank was named Matilda after a cartoon duck it somewhat resembled! The pilot model was built in 1936, following a General Staff Requirement for a tank to support the infantry. Although it was armed with a single machine gun, its 10–60 mm armour, compared with 6–14 mm on the cruiser tank, made it invulnerable to enemy anti-tank fire in the early war years. Indeed, it was the Matilda Is and IIs which were the only tanks capable of holding up Rommel's Panzer Division in their drive for the Channel ports in 1940. With a crew of two, this little 11-tonner waddled along at 8 mph.

3 DEVELOPMENTS BETWEEN THE WARS

French

Renault FT Kegresse light tank. In an attempt to modernise the highly successful Renault FT a new running gear was fitted, which made the tank faster and also quieter. The photograph shows one of the Renault FTs fitted with the Citroën-Kegresse running gear, whilst under test with the US Army who had also shown interest in the idea. Its weight was about 6.4 tons, the main armament was one 37 mm gun or one machine gun. It could travel at about 7½ mph. It was also known as the M24/25.

Heavy tank Char 2C. During World War I the French had issued a specification for a heavy 'breakthrough' tank, Char de Rupture C, at a weight of about 40 tons. Two prototypes, Chars 1A and 1B were produced in 1917–18. Then, later development produced an even heavier tank – nearly 70 tons in weight. This was the Char 2C. It did not become operational during the war, but ten were built, the last being delivered in 1922. In their day they were the most powerful tanks in the world, with a crew of twelve, a 75 mm gun in the front turret and four machine gun (one in an auxiliary turret at the rear of the tank). One of them was converted to mount a 155 mm howitzer as well as the 75 mm and the four machine guns and led some Intelligence circles to think that France was building large numbers of 'super tanks'. The Char 2C had two 250 hp Mercedes engines driving electric generators to run a motor for each track and give the tank a top speed of 8 mph. The last of these tanks were destroyed in 1940 by air attack, when they were being transported to the front by train.

Char léger AMR33 light tank. AMR standing for 'Auto-mitrailleuse de Reconnaissance', this type of 5-ton tank was mainly used by recce troops. It had a crew of two, mounted a 7.5 mm machine gun and had a top speed of over 30 mph. This pair of AMR33 are taking part in Bastille Day celebrations in Paris on 14 June 1935, with President Lebrun taking the salute.

Char léger AMR35 light tank. Following on from the AMR33, Renault produced their AMR35 ZT model, which was very similar, but with more powerful armament (one 13.2 mm and one 7.5 mm machine guns), improved vision devices, and other features including a better suspension. Some 200 AMR35 were built and widely used.

Char léger H39 light tank (*Above*). The Char léger H39 (Hotchkiss) was an infantry tank as opposed to the cavalry vehicles of the last two photographs. It was the last of the Hotchkiss light tanks (its predecessors were the H35 and H38). It had a crew of two, mounted a long barrelled 37 mm gun and had a top speed of 17.5 mph. It was used by the Free French and by the Germans during World War 2.

Char léger FCM36 Infantry tank (*Centre right*). A 12-ton tank produced in 1936 with a 37 mm gun and a machine gun in an octagonal shaped turret, which had a non-rotating commanders position on the top. It was designed for the purpose of accompanying infantry. Powered by a 90 hp Berliet water-cooled engine, it had a top speed of 15 mph and a radius of action of about 200 miles. Some 100 were built and saw action in 1940. Many were captured by the Germans who continued to use them thereafter.

Char D1 Infantry tank (*Right*). One of the first tanks in the world to be fitted with a cast turret, this infantry tank (medium) first appeared as the D1A in 1931, which was a 12-tonner, with a crew of three, mounting a 37 mm gun; then as the D1B which mounted a 47 mm gun and had thicker armoured plate. One feature was the large aerial mounted behind the turret. Most of the Char D1 were deployed in North Africa.

Renault Chenillette d'Infanterie supply carrier (*Above left*). Inspired by the Carden-Loyd Mark V, the Type UE supply carrier normally towed a small supply trailer as seen in this photograph. It had a crew of two, weighed just under 2 tons and first entered service in the French Army in 1931. Its 35 hp engine gave it a road speed of 18 mph. Large numbers of these supporting carriers were captured by the Germans when France fell in 1940 and were then used in their service mainly as ammunition carriers (Gepanzerter Munitionsschlepper).

Char B1 heavy tank (*Above right*). The B1 appeared in 1935 with 60 mm of armour and a top speed of 17 mph. This 31-ton tank was in its day one of the most formidable tanks in the world. The B1 *bis* version seen in the photograph evolved from the B1; it had thicker armour, a larger gun in the turret (47 mm instead of 37 mm) and a more powerful engine. Like the B1 its main armament was a 75 mm gun in a hull mounting to the right and below the drivers position. No traverse was possible for this weapon, so to lay in azimuth the tank had to be turned on its tracks.

Char S35 Somua medium tank. Another good tank, with all cast construction of both hull and turret. Main armament was a long barrelled 47 mm gun with a co-axial machine gun. Some 500 of these 20-tonners were built and, like all contemporary French tanks, were captured in large numbers by the Germans and then used in their service. Its 190 hp engine gave the S35 a top speed of 25 mph and a radius of action of 160 miles. Fast and reliable, it was better armed and better armoured than its German opponents in 1940.

French tank production. A good photograph of a French tank factory assembly lines in full swing as they turn out heavy tanks by the score. The French had some 4,500 tanks of all types in the summer of 1940, yet the German armour was able to outmanoeuvre and outfight them with ease.

American

Cunningham light tank (*Above*). A one-man tank built in 1928, with flexible tracks made of steel bands and transmission belting. It weighed only 1½ tons and had a top speed of 20 mph.

M1922 medium tank (*Top left*). Between 1921 and 1925, the Americans built three prototype medium tanks – Medium A of 1921, Medium A of 1922 (pictured here) and T1 in 1925. All had British influence in their design, for example the M1922 incorporated the flexible tracks of the Medium D. All weighed over 20 tons, mounted a 37 mm gun and machine gun (no armament fitted in photograph). They did not go into production as the intended programme, like all American tank development, was hamstrung by lack of money.

T2 medium tank. This tank appeared in 1920 and in external appearance resembled the British Vickers medium. With a 300 hp engine and a weight of only about 13 tons, it had excellent power to weight ratio. Main armament was now a 47 mm gun. Later medium tanks – T3, T3E2 and T4 – were all built to J. Walter Christie's designs (see later) but never got further than the prototype stage.

T1E2 light tank. One of a number of versions of the light tank T1, built in 1928–29. It was a two-man tank, mounting a 37 mm gun and a machine gun in the turret, which gave it considerably better armament than its contemporaries in other nations which were generally only armed with machine guns.

Light tanks M2A2 and M2A3 (*Above left*). Light tanks of the US Army are seen here on training at Camp Beauregard, Louisiana in early 1941. With their double turrets they were known as 'Mae Wests' by the tankers for obvious anatomical reasons! The light tank that followed, the M2A4 was based, as far as the turret is concerned, on the Cavalry Combat Cars, rather than the infantry tanks.

Combat Car M1 (*Above right*). The title 'Combat Car' was adopted to get round the difficulty of anyone having tanks except for the infantry! This car appeared in 1935, intended for use by the mechanised cavalry, and mounted three machine guns, two in the turret (.50 and .30) and another .30 in the hull. There was also another machine gun on an AA mounting – the first recorded use of this on any tank.

Marmon-Herrington light tank T16. Between 1935 and 1941, the Marmon-Herrington Co. Inc., produced a series of tanks, mainly for export. One of the later models was the CTLS-4TAC seen here, also called the light tank T16. It was built for export to the Dutch East Indies, which is where the photograph was taken. It had a two-man crew, weighed about 8½ tons and was armed with machine guns only. A number of these tanks were used for training by the US Army.

Medium tank M2. In August 1939 production of fifteen of these medium tanks was authorised at Rock Island Arsenal. Main armament of this 19-ton, six-man tank, was a 37 mm gun. It also had no less than eight machine guns (not fitted on this vehicle, which is seen on a test track). It was powered by a 350 hp air-cooled radial engine and was the tank from which the M3 Grant and Lee and the famous Sherman M4 evolved during World War 2.

J. Walter Christie (*Above*). Tank development between the wars owed much to the brilliant, but unpredictable American engineer J. Walter Christie, who was the advocate of light, fast tanks that could move cross country at amazing speeds on his unique suspension system. The tanks could run equally well without their tracks, on road wheels. Although the US Army did not take up his designs in a big way, other countries showed far more interest, as the photographs on this and the next page show. Here Christie himself drives one of his medium tanks, the T3.

A Christie tank (*Top left*). This example demonstrates its ability to run on its wheels, while on test.

Christie M1932 (*Centre left*). Showing off its high speed whilst leaping a ditch, is one of a series of fast tanks Christie designed and built between 1928 and 1932. It is reputed to have had a top speed, on its tracks, of over 40 mph, while on its wheels on roads it could reach 70 mph! Two of these tanks were purchased by the Russians and became models for the BT series (see later).

Medium tank T3 (*Bottom left*). The US Army did accept a small number of Christie tanks into service, although they did not like his business methods! The tank had a 37 mm and co-axial machine gun in a fully traversing turret and weighed about 11 tons. *Hurricane* could travel at over 45 mph on its wheels and 27 mph on its tracks.

51

Russian BT tank (*Top left*). The BT1 medium tank was copied from the M1931 which had been bought by Russia from the USA, a Christie design. It was powered by an engine copied from the American Liberty engine.

British Cruiser tank Mark IVA (*Centre left*). This up-armoured version of the A13 had, like its predecessor, a Christie suspension, which gave it a high speed – 30 mph. This particular tank is being used to raise funds for Westminster's 'War Weapons Week'.

Christie M1937 (*Below*). Looking like something out of the space age, this armoured 6-tonner, which was offered to Britain, had a small conical cupola on the front glacis plate and front idlers on bracketed stub shafts.

3 DEVELOPMENTS BETWEEN THE WARS

Russian

MS light tank. Although the Russians now claim that they invented the tank, the first Russian tanks were actually the British heavy Mark Vs and French Renault FTs, bought by the Imperial Government in 1918 and then taken over by the Bolsheviks. They acquired more Mark Vs (they called them Ricardos) from the BEF when they withdrew. The first Russian-built tank was a copy of the Renault, the KS (Krasno-Sormova, after the place where it was built), but also called the 'Russki-Renault'. It was later followed by a Soviet designed MS series (Maliy Soprovozdieniya, meaning 'little tank that accompanies'). The MS series were built by the Bolshevik factory, Leningrad, weighed about 7 tons, and were armed with a 37 mm gun and a machine gun. Some MS and Ricardos are seen here on a May Day parade in Moscow.

T27 tankette (*Above*). This was the Russian version of the Carden-Loyd Mark VI. It was used in place of a light tank. Some 4,000 were built. It had thin, overhead cover for its two-man crew and mounted a single machine gun. After 1933 they were relegated to the training role or used as gun towers, but had played a significant part in teaching the Army the use of armour.

T26 light tank series (*Above right*). The T26 was based on the Vickers 6-ton tank, with initially two basic models (A – twin turrets, B – single turret). Later variations, the T26C series, were more Russian in design (see next page). The T26A-2 had 7.62 mm machine guns and weighed about $8\frac{1}{2}$ tons.

T37 Amphibious light tank (*Right*). Another 'acquired' design, based upon the Vickers Carden-Loyd amphibious tank purchased from Britain in 1928–29. It was copied and came into service as the T37 and T37A. Both were armed with one machine gun in a revolving turret on the right.

T26C light tank series (*Opposite top left*). The end of the T26 series was the T26C and the photograph shows one, its redesigned turret and thicker armour very evident, as is the high velocity 45 mm gun now mounted as main armament. These new features put the weight up to nearly $10\frac{1}{2}$ tons.

BT light tank series (*Opposite top right*). In 1931, the Soviets obtained some M31 Christie tanks with the aim of developing a tank with a better speed and cross country performance than the T26. From the prototype evolved the BT (Bystrochodya tank – literally 'fast tank') series, the photograph showing the BT3. At between 10.2 and 15.6 tons, dependent upon model, the BT was approaching the medium range and is classified thus in some books. The BT3 mounted a 47 mm gun instead of the original 37 mm as main armament.

BT7 light tank (*Bottom left*). First produced in 1935, the BT7 weighed 13.8 tons, mounted a 45 mm gun and had a top speed of 33 mph. It was widely used at the start of World War 2. It had 20 mm thick armour, an increase of 7 mm over the previous version. The BT7M, produced in 1939, had a 500 hp engine with a top speed of over 40 mph and a range of 375 miles, which was achieved using jettison tanks – a far greater range than any contemporary AFV.

T28 medium tank (*Top right*). Various models were built of this 'exploitation' tank, which resembled the British A1E1 Independent externally, but had only two additional machine gun turrets instead of four. The T28 weighed about $27\frac{1}{2}$ tons. Later models mounted the more powerful 76.2 mm howitzer in place of the prototype's 45 mm gun. The tank was used in the Russo-Finnish war.

T35 heavy tank (*Centre right*). In 1932 a requirement arose for a heavy tank to deal with enemy infantry and anti-tank weapons (*cf*: Char 2C) and during the next seven years various models of the T35 heavy tank were produced. Weighing some 45 tons, it was well armed with a 76.2 mm howitzer in the main turret, plus four subsidiary turrets, of which, the off-side front and near-side rear mounted a 45 mm gun each, and the other two, a machine gun each.

SMK heavy tank (*Bottom right*). Named after the Soviet political leader Sergei Mironovich Kirov, who was assassinated in 1934, this tank was a complete departure from normal Soviet design. The hull had eight suspension wheels on either side, with torsion bar springing and four return rollers. There was an upper and lower turret, with a 76.2 mm gun in the top turret and a 45 mm in the lower. It had a crew of seven, weighed 45 tons and had armour up to 60 mm thick. It closely resembled the T100 heavy tank which appeared in 1938, a year after the SMK and weighed 11 tons more. Both were used in the Russo-Finnish war when this photograph was taken.

55

3 DEVELOPMENTS BETWEEN THE WARS

Italian

Fiat 3000 light tank (*Below left*). In 1918, France supplied Italy with a small number of Renault FT17s and these were copied by Fiat, using Italian parts. The first prototype model appeared in 1920, but did not enter service with the Italian Army until 1923. Various models were produced between then and 1930. They remained in service until the middle of World War 2. Weighing about 6 tons, the tank was initially armed with machine guns, but the 1930 model had a 37 mm, while the Fiat 3000B (modified) had twin 37 mm guns in the turret – see photograph. The AFV in front of the Fiat is a Carro Veloce CV33 tankette which is described next.

Carro Veloce 33 tankette (*Above*). In 1929 the Italians purchased some Vickers-Carden-Loyd Mk VI tankettes and at the same time obtained permission to manufacture them in Italy. A total of 25 was built under the designation Carro Veloce 29 by Ansaldo, with automotive parts from Fiat. The CV33 was directly descended from the CV29, designed and built by Ansaldo in 1931–32. There were various models over the years of this little $3\frac{1}{4}$-ton two-man tankette and armament was either one or two machine guns. The photograph shows the CV33/11, with twin machine guns.

CV33/11 bridgelayer (*Left*). In 1936, the Italian Engineers converted a small number of CV33s into bridgelayers (Carro Veloce Passerella). They were never used in combat, but were clearly of great interest on demonstrations!

L35 flamethrower (*Below*). A graphic photograph of the flamethrower variant of the tankette which had a long-barrelled hooded flamethrower instead of the usual machine guns. A 500-litre armoured fuel trailer was towed behind the 'carro lanciafiamme'. On a later model the flamethrower fuel tank was mounted on the rear of the vehicle.

Carro Armato M13/40 medium tank (*Bottom right*). Although this medium tank evolved from the M11/39, it was better in every respect. It was probably the best most widely used Italian tank of World War 2, although, to put it into perspective, it must be said that Italian tanks were inferior to their opponents – this one was no match, for example, for the British Matilda II. The M13/40 was armed with a 47 mm gun, weighed 14 tons and had a 125 hp engine which gave it a road speed of 20 mph. Nearly 2,000 were built.

Carro Armato M11/39 medium tank (*Above*). At 11 tons, this was the beginning of the Italian medium tank line, evolved from earlier, lighter versions. The main armament was a 37 mm gun mounted in the front of the hull, with twin machine guns in the small manually operated turret which was offset to the left. Powered by a V-8 105 hp engine, it had very thin armour and was of little use in battle, so when it went into action in North Africa in 1940 against the British, it was quickly knocked out.

Carro Armato P26/40 heavy tank (*Left*). Only about twenty of these 26-ton tanks were built before the Italians surrendered in September 1943, so there is little combat experience on which to assess its performance. It had a 75 mm gun as main armament and considerably thicker armour than the M13/40. A few were taken over and used by the Germans.

Semovente 75/18 SU M40 self-propelled gun. Although not strictly a tank, the M40 SP gun was based upon the chassis of the M13/40 and was an excellent weapon, widely used in support of armoured divisions in North Africa and Sicily. After the Italian surrender, the Germans continued to use them in considerable numbers. The 75 mm howitzer could traverse 25° either side of the centre line, and was mounted in a simple boxlike structure which replaced the turret.

The Duce inspects his armoured might. Benito Mussolini, Italian Dictator, rides proudly past a line of his little tank-ettes. They were of little use in battle, being quickly knocked out by the British.

3 DEVELOPMENTS BETWEEN THE WARS

Polish

Tankette TK S. TK1 led on to TK2 and TK3, the last named being modified during the 1930s to mount a 20 mm cannon. An up-armoured version of the TK3, was the TK S produced in 1933, which was armed with a single ball-mounted machine gun. The driver was on the left of this 2½-ton vehicle. Some 400 were built and fought against the Germans when they invaded Poland, but were no match for the Nazi *panzers*. Some were used later by the Germans.

Tankette TK1. Yet another tankette that owes its origin to the Vickers Carden-Loyd Mark VI is the Polish TK1, seen on the left of this photograph. The Poles obtained some Carden-Loyds from Britain (those can be seen at the other end of the row) and then developed a series of their own tankettes from 1929 onwards.

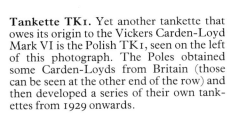

Light tank 7TP with twin turret (*Bottom*). In addition to the Carden-Loyds, another British export was the ubiquitous Vickers 6-ton Mark E model, which was copied by the Poles who produced the 7TP, a 9-ton twin-turreted light tank, which was armed with a variety of machine guns – Brownings, Maxims and Hotchkiss. It was powered by a 110 hp diesel engine.

Light tank 7TP with single turret (*Below*). The twin turret of the first model was soon replaced by a single turret from Sweden which mounted a Bofors 37 mm gun. About 160 of this model were built. They came into production in 1937 and a few were used by the Germans, after Poland was overrun.

Vickers 6-ton in Polish service. Dressed in a striking pattern of camouflage, this single turreted Vickers 6-tonner was one of a number of single and twin-turreted light tanks sold to the Poles in the 1930s, which, together with the Carden-Loyd carriers, could be said to be the real beginnings of the Polish armoured corps, although much earlier in 1920, they had received a few Renault tanks during the Russo-Polish war. The Poles went on to design medium and even heavy tanks, but these never got further than the drawing board.

3 DEVELOPMENTS BETWEEN THE WARS

Japanese

Ot-su A1923 (Type Koh) – Renault light tanks in Japanese service. Japanese interest in tanks began in the early 1920s, when they bought various foreign tanks – British Mark Vs and Whippets, French Renault FTs and NCIs – for evaluation. Other purchases included the Vickers Medium C and Carden-Loyd tankettes. These Renaults, some of which were still in service in 1940, are pictured in Manchuria in 1936.

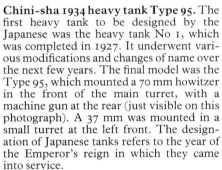

Chini-sha 1934 heavy tank Type 95. The first heavy tank to be designed by the Japanese was the heavy tank No 1, which was completed in 1927. It underwent various modifications and changes of name over the next few years. The final model was the Type 95, which mounted a 70 mm howitzer in the front of the main turret, with a machine gun at the rear (just visible on this photograph). A 37 mm was mounted in a small turret at the left front. The designation of Japanese tanks refers to the year of the Emperor's reign in which they came into service.

Type 94 tankette. Like so many other countries, the Japanese bought several Vickers Carden-Loyd Mark VIs and from these developed their own tankettes. However, unlike the Mark VI, these had a small turret, mounting a single machine gun. It came into service in 1934 and two years later a modified version was produced with a trailing idler. Further adaptation gave rise to a diesel version. It is interesting to note that the Japanese were ahead of all other countries in their dieselisation programme, which not only reduced the risk of fire, but also lowered fuel consumption and obviated the need for higher grade fuel.

Type 97 Te-Ke/Ke-Ke tankette. Last of the Japanese tankette line was the Type 97 which entered service in 1938. It was armed with a 37 mm gun for which 97 rounds were carried. Thicker armour and a more powerful engine pushed the weight up by over a ton to 4.7 tons. Although production continued during World War 2 and it was built in larger numbers than any other Japanese tankette, it was really obsolete in 1940.

Type 95 Ha-Go light tank. One of the best tanks to be built by the Japanese, the Ha-Go saw action in China and then throughout the Far East in World War 2. Some 1,250 were built of this 7½-ton light tank, which had a crew of three and a 37 mm gun as its main armament. A bow machine gunner sat next to the driver, so the commander had to load, aim and fire the main gun by himself. Powered by a 110 hp diesel engine, the Ha-Go had a top speed of 25 mph.

Type 89B Ot-Su medium tank. Having obtained, as previously mentioned, a Vickers Medium C from Britain, the Japanese Osaka Arsenal produced a Type 89 light tank at just under 10 tons, mounting a 57 mm gun and two machine guns. They were so delighted with its design that they used it as the basis for a heavier, medium tank (Type 89) which was standardised in 1929. From 1936, a diesel version of this tank, the Type 89B, was developed by Mitsubishi and remained in service most of World War 2. There were two versions; the first is seen in this photograph, which has a one-piece front plate, the driver being located on the left. Main armament was a Type 90 57 mm gun and there was a machine gun at the rear of the turret, plus another on the right of the front plate.

Type 97 Chi-Ha medium tank. Probably the most successful of all Japanese tank designs, the Chi-Ha saw service throughout World War 2, having been selected for mass production in 1937. However, it was no match for the Sherman or other Allied medium tanks. It was armed with a 57 mm gun and two machine guns, one of which was mounted, as the photograph clearly shows, at the rear of the turret. With a crew of four, this 15-ton tank was powered by 170 hp air-cooled diesel engine and had a top speed of 24 mph.

Type 89B Ot-Su medium tank – other model. Another model of this medium tank had the driver's position and machine gun reversed, while the front plate was all in one piece. The skirting plates had also been redesigned, with four return rollers in place of the five girder mounted return rollers of the previous model.

Type 2 Ka-Mi amphibious tank. Based upon the Ha-Go light tank, the Ka-Mi was the most successful Japanese amphibious tank. The Japanese had long been interested in amphibious armoured vehicles for use by their Imperial Navy. The Ka-Mi had two detachable floats, one at the bow and one at the stern, which gave the tank its buoyancy whilst in the water. Once it came ashore, these could be discarded. The tank was driven through the water by means of two propellers worked off the main engine, while the tank commander could steer via twin rudders which he operated from his turret. Main armament was a 37 mm gun. The tank carried additional crewmen to the Ha-Go (five instead of three). There was a slightly larger and heavier version designed, the Type 5 Ko-Tu, which weighed just over 29 tons and mounted a 47 mm gun, but did not go into production. All up weight of the Ka-Mi with pontoons was $12\frac{1}{2}$ tons.

3 DEVELOPMENTS BETWEEN THE WARS

Swedish

Strv M/21–29. Despite the fact that Sweden has not taken part in any war this century, they still kept up with the development of armoured fighting vehicles, having begun in 1921 with a copy of the German Leichte Kampfwagen. This is hardly surprising, as it was designed by J. Vollmer, the German engineer, who built and designed the LKII, and moved to Sweden after the war. The Strv (Stridsvagn – 'tank') M/21 was built in 1921, while the one pictured here was the 1929 rebuild, which had a more powerful engine and heavier armour.

Strv M/31 light tank. By the late 1920s, with German assistance, the Swedes had established their own tank factory, the AB Landsverk Company at Landskrons. Their first design, which appeared in 1929, was a wheel/track vehicle, with duplicate running gear. Two years later they produced the Strv M/31, which was, in design, well in advance of other nations, the turret and hull both being of welded construction. Main armament of this four man, $11\frac{1}{2}$-ton tank, was a 37 mm gun. Its engine was a German Bussing 140 hp V-6. It was also known as the L-10 light tank.

Strv fm/31 wheel and track light tank. Also known as the L-30, this light tank was developed at the same time as the M/31, incorporating the same turret. Although this tank was not put into full production, it was tested exhaustively and the changeover from wheels to tracks or *vice versa* could be achieved in under half a minute – even when the tank was moving!

Strv m/37 light tank. Despite their interest in armoured fighting vehicles, the Swedes did not begin to mechanise their army until the mid-1930s and then chose a foreign tank in preference to their own models. This was the Czechoslovakian 4½-ton light tank AH-IV-Sv, built under licence. Some 50 Strv m/37, as they were called in Sweden, were sent in pieces by the Czechs and assembled in Sweden.

Strv m/39 light tank (*Left*). This well designed 9-ton light tank was developed from earlier models at the Landsknona factory, and produced in 1939. It had a 37 mm gun as main armament and two machine guns. Another feature was the use of steering levers to replace the steering wheel of the previous m/38 model.

Strv m/41 light tank (*Above*). Another Czech designed light tank, built under licence by the Swedes. The m/41s continued in service with the Swedish Army until the 1950s and then many were modified for use as armoured personnel carriers. Some 240 of these 10½-ton light tanks were in service.

Strv m/42 medium tank. This was the first Swedish tank to mount a 75 mm gun. It entered service in 1944, weighed 22½ tons and had a four man crew. In the late 1950s, the m/42s were rebuilt as the Strv 74, with a more powerful gun and better armour.

Miscellaneous

Belgium: T15 light tank (*Below*). This was the Belgian designation for the British M1934 light tank, built under licence by Fabrique National of Belgium. It was used to equip the Belgian Army, along with various other models of similar Carden-Loyd light tanks. It was armed with a 13.2 mm Hotchkiss machine gun. Some 40 T15s were built.

Afghanistan: Disston tractor from USA (*Above left*). Three of these commercial caterpillar tractors with armoured bodies were sold to Afghanistan in 1936. They were armed with a 37 mm gun in an open topped turret, plus a machine gun in the front plate. They weighed nearly 7 tons and had a top speed of about $4\frac{1}{2}$ mph.

Austria: AIMK Motorkarette (*Centre left*). Also called 'Mulus', this small wheel and track carrier came into service in 1935. It was used basically to carry a single machine gun (*cf*: the Bren carrier). Various successive models followed over the next few years. However, from the *Anschluss* with Germany in 1938, largely Nazi equipment was used.

Brazil: CV33 tankette (*Bottom left*). Brazil acquired some of these Italian-built Fiat CV33 tankettes, armed with a Madsen 13.2 mm machine gun.

Finland: Vickers Armstrong 6-ton light tank (*Right*). Just before World War 2, Finland bought various British light tanks and tankettes, including 27 of these 6-ton Mark E Vickers-Armstrong light tanks. They were modified in Finland and fitted with Swedish Landsverk turrets, mounting a Bofors 37 mm gun.

Czechoslovakia: S-IIb CKD V8H. The Prague based firm Ceskomoravska Kolben Danek (CKD) begun to construct its own light tanks in the early 1930s and were quite successful in selling various models to other countries as well as equipping their own forces with some 400 tanks and tankettes by 1939. The photograph shows a model produced in 1938 which was developed from their LT34 5-ton light tank.

Hungary: Turan 1. The first tanks in Hungary were Italian. They later purchased various models from the Czech firm of Weiss and Csepel of Budapest. The Turan 1, seen here, was built by Weiss and Csepel under licence from Landsverk AB of Sweden, with a squarish turret mounting a 40 mm gun and machine gun, with another in the hull. There were two later models (Turan II and III) which both mounted a 75 mm gun.

Lithuania: Carden-Loyd M1936 (*Top left*). The Lithuanians purchased some eighteen of these British light tanks in 1937.

Spain: T26 light tank (*Above*). During the Spanish Civil War, the Loyalist armoured forces were mainly armed with Russian tanks, such as this T26 light tank.

Spain: Landesa ad hoc tank (*Centre left*). Built in 1934, this experimental armoured hull on an agricultural tractor was very similar to the US Disston tank (see earlier photograph). It was armed with a machine gun in the rear cab.

Spain: Pzkfpw 1 light tank (*Above*). On the other side, the Nationalists were equipped with German and Italian AFVs, such as these little 5½-ton German light tanks, armed with twin machine guns. The photograph shows Nationalist tanks moving up through a street in Grandella during Franco's great offensive in Catalonia.

Romania: LT35 (*Bottom left*). Seen here on parade are Skoda light tanks LT35, which were purchased in 1936–37 from Czechoslovakia. The main armament of this 10½-ton tank was a 37 mm gun.

Thailand (Siam): Vickers-Armstrong 6-ton light tank. The ubiquitous Vickers-Armstrong 6-ton Mark E (seen here) and the Carden-Loyd tankettes, even got as far as Siam in the 1930s, as this photograph shows.

Yugoslavia: S-Id tankette. Yet another Czech-built AFV, this tankette was built in 1938 for Yugoslavia and later used by Romania. At 4½ tons, it was heavy for a tankette and mounted a 47 mm gun.

Goodbye to Boots and Saddles! An M2A4, belonging to the 7th US Cavalry Brigade (Mechanised) overtakes a column of horsemen during US Army exercises in the summer of 1940. In a few years America would produce more armoured fighting vehicles than any other country in the world.

World War Two
4 Germany

At the end of World War 1, the Treaty of Versailles banned tank production in postwar Germany along with that of most other weapons of war. However, some work did continue in secret and a few tanks were designed and built, being called *'Traktoren'* to disguise their true identity. Once the Nazis came to power, all such subterfuge was swept aside and the Germans began to design and build tanks quite openly. Their heavy manufacturing industry was only too happy to oblige, while their soldiers seized avidly on the ideas of British tank pioneers such as Liddel Hart, Fuller and Hobart, in planning ways to use these new weapons to their best advantage. Panzer divisions were formed and the tactical handling of armour practised at all levels. The Germans used the Spanish Civil War as a testing ground for their new AFVs and refined their tactical ideas as each new annexation swallowed up more and more 'living space' in Europe. Throughout these conquests the Panzer Divisions acted as the spearhead to the *Blitzkrieg*, spreading terror and destruction in their path.

In their tank design, the Germans concentrated on that most important of all tank characteristics, namely *firepower*, rightly appreciating that if they armed their tanks with better tank guns than the Allies, then they were bound to stay ahead in tank *versus* tank warfare. And so it was throughout the whole of World War 2, German tanks, with very few exceptions, were always able to outgun their opponents, both in range and lethality. In addition, they rightly appreciated the need for a dual purpose main gun, just as capable of firing HE to take on the anti-tank gun and dismounted infantry as of knocking out enemy tanks with AP. Machine guns were added to save needless expenditure of main armament rounds. Up to and including the Tiger 1, German tanks all had a very square-looking profile, with the armour plates at right angles to the horizontal. Extra protection was gained by fitting spaced armour, such as anti-bazooka screens, or by bolting on extra thicknesses of plate. Their shock meeting with the Russian T34 tank had a profound effect upon German tank design, a special commission being set up to look for ways of combating this threat to their superiority. It is interesting to see how much notice they took of the sloping shape of the T34, which is reflected in later German designs, such as the Panther and Royal Tiger.

In addition to manufacturing bigger and better tank guns, the Germans built bigger and heavier tanks, as the battle became, for them, a more defensive one. The 56-ton Tiger was joined by the 70-ton Royal Tiger and the even more enormous JagdTiger, while the gigantic Maus, weighing in at 188 tons, just failed to get into production before the war entered its final phase and the Allies reached the very heart of the Fatherland. Mobility came a poor third after firepower and protection, so it is surprising to see the switch in postwar German tank design, when Leopard I relied more on its speed than on armour for its basic protection.

During World War 2 German tanks established a reputation of invincibility that far outweighed their actual numbers – the Americans, for example, produced twice as many Sherman gun tanks alone as the *entire* German wartime tank production. However, the quality of the German tanks and their tank crews was, at the start of the war anyway, far superior to the Allies and as such they undoubtedly showed the world how armour should be used.

Pzkpfw III Ausf J medium tank. The Pzkpfw III and IV medium tanks were the mainstays of the German Panzer Divisions during World War 2. More Ausf Js were produced than of any other Pzkpfw III, over 1,500 being manufactured between early 1941 and mid-1942. It was the first Pzkpfw III to have thicker frontal armour – up to 50 mm – which put the combat weight up to 21½ tons. The Pzkpfw III Ausf J in this photograph was serving with Rommel's Deutsche Afrika Korps in North Africa.

German Light Tanks

Pzkpfw I Ausf A light tank (*Left*). Military parade in Berlin, 21 April 1936. Panzerkampfwagen (Pzkpfw) Ausf A lined up along the Unter den Linden, waiting for Adolf Hitler to inspect them. The Pzkpfw I Ausf A was the first German tank to go into mass production. It had the same hull and suspension as its predecessor, the Pzkpfw I Ausf A ohne Aufbau (literally 'without turret') which had been produced without a turret and weapon system to get around the Treaty of Versailles which prevented Germany from having tanks. Weighing only $5\frac{1}{2}$ tons, with a crew of two and mounting two 7.92 mm machine guns, it was soon outclassed on the battlefield and was withdrawn from active service in 1941.

Pzkpfw I Ausf B light tank (*Above*). The Ausf B had a slightly longer chassis than the Ausf A (just under .5 m longer) and a more powerful engine. The modification put its weight up to 5.8 tons. It was also phased out of service in 1941.

Kleiner Panzerbefehlswagen command tank (*Below*). This was the command version of the Pzkpfw I. It was used at company, battalion, regimental and brigade level in the headquarters of panzer units from the mid-1930s up to the early war years. A radio transmitter was included in addition to the radio receiver normally only fitted in the Pzkpfw I. The superstructure had to be raised in height to make room for the radio and the third crew member – the radio operator.

Ladunsleger (demolition charge layer). This version of the Pzkpfw I Ausf B had an odd looking cable operated arm which could drop a demolition charge over the rear end of the tank. This could be placed near obstacles and then set off remotely.

Panzerjager 4.7 cm PaK(t) self-propelled anti-tank gun. This was an adaptation of the Pzkpfw I, the basic Ausf B having been modified to accept a 4.7 cm PaK anti-tank gun. About 200 were converted to this role. Another self-propelled version mounted a 15 cm heavy infantry gun on to the Ausf B. The 4.7 PaK(t) weighed 6.4 tons, the 15 cm sIG33 $8\frac{1}{2}$ tons.

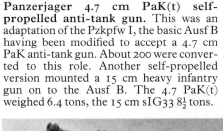

Pzkpfw II Ausf A light tank (*Below right*). The next model in the German light tank family was the Pzkpfw II and the photograph shows the final development model in a series of three (A, B and C), by which time the suspension had changed from one very similar to the Pzkpfw I to five independently sprung, larger roadwheels and four top rollers. Weighing nearly 9 tons, the three-man tank was armed with a 2 cm gun and one MG34. The A version is distinguishable from later models by the periscope on the turret top placed centrally behind the guns. No cupola was fitted.

Pzkpfw I Ausf F heavy assault tank. Final development of the Pzkpfw I was this 21-ton model, an infantry assault tank, which had very thick armour, up to 80 mm on the turret as compared with 13 mm on the Ausf A. Thirty were built in 1942, and a few were subsequently taken to Russia for combat testing. However, as a result of these tests further orders were cancelled. The armament of the two-man tank was only two MG34.

Blitzkrieg in action (*Above*). A 7.5 cm infantry gun is moved into position, while Pzkpfw IIs mass behind it for the last onslaught on Warsaw. The city fell on 27 September 1939, after a campaign that lasted only 28 days, during which 58 German divisions, including fourteen panzer divisions, were opposed by much weaker Polish forces with only one motorised division.

Pzkpfw II Ausf B and C light tank (*Left*). Compared to the model A, only minor variations have been made, which include extra bolted-on armour plate and a cupola. Watched by General Erwin Rommel – 'The Desert Fox' (right) – this Pzkpfw II is being unloaded in Tripoli docks at the start of German involvement with the African campaigns.

Flammpanzer II – flamethrower. Also called 'Flamingo', this light flamethrowing tank was an adaptation of the Pzkpfw II, which had two flamethrowers mounted on the front corners of the tank's superstructure. This particular tank is shown under test by the Russians who captured it near Leningrad.

Pzkpfw II Ausf F light tank. A good rear view of the last model of the Pzkpfw II original series, some 500 of which were produced. It had better armour which put up the weight by ½ ton, but its armament remained the same.

7.62 cm PaK(r) auf Fgst Pzkpfw II(Sf) SP anti-tank gun. Produced in early 1942 and based on the Pzkpfw II Model D and E, this self-propelled anti-tank gun (Panzer Jaeger) mounted a Russian 7.62 cm gun which had been captured in large quantities early on in the Russian campaign. Later, the gun was rechambered to take the PaK40 round and fitted with a muzzle brake, as seen here.

15 cm sIG33 auf Fgst Pzkpfw II(Sf) heavy SP gun. Only twelve of these self-propelled guns were produced in late 1941, the chassis being that of a Pzkpfw II which had been slightly widened and lengthened so as to make room for the gun. As the photograph shows, this meant adding a sixth roadwheel on each side.

Panzerspahwagen II light recce tank. Also called 'Luchs' (Lynx), this AFV was designed and developed as a reconnaissance tank. It had a crew of four and weighed 13 tons. Its main armament was a 2 cm KwK38 gun, with a coaxially mounted MG34. About 100 were built in late 1943 and saw service in both Russia and Europe.

Wespe (Sd Kfz 124) SP light field howitzer (*Left*). About 700 Wasps were produced in 1943–44. They mounted the 10.5 cm le FH18M light field howitzer. They proved to be a most effective SP and saw active service on all fronts.

Pzkpfw 38(t) light tank (*Below left*). Produced in Czechoslovakia for the German Army after the annexation of Bohemia and Moravia in 1939 the Pzkpfw 38(t) mounted a 3.7 cm gun plus two machine guns. The photograph shows the Ausf E version, at the school of Tank Technology, taken in August 1942.

Pz Jag 38(t) fur 7.62 cm PaK36(r) SP anti-tank gun (*Below*). Also known as Marder III (Marten), this was another conversion of a tank to take the Russian 7.62 cm gun, this time mounting it on a Czech-produced Pzkpfw 38(t) light tank, which was too light to be much use on the battlefield by 1941. Most of these Pz Jag 38s were in action on the Russian front, although a small number served in North Africa.

7.5 cm PaK 40/2 auf Fgst Pzkpfw II SP anti-tank gun (*Left*). One of the most widely used German self-propelled anti-tank guns was this version of the Pzkpfw II to carry the 7.5 cm PaK 40/2. By mid-June 1942 it had been decided that the Pzkpfw II was not adequate for combat, so all production was diverted to producing SP guns. Over 500 7.5 cm PaK 40/2 were issued to Panzer Jaeger units and remained in service until the end of the war.

15 cm sIG33(Sf) auf Pzkpfw 38(t) Aus H SP heavy gun (*Right*). This 11½-ton self-propelled infantry heavy gun was also called Grille (Cricket). It served on most battlefronts, and had a crew of five.

7.5 cm PaK40/3 auf Pzkpfw 38(t) Ausf H SP anti-tank gun (*Below*). Designed as the replacement for the 7.62 cm Marder III, this SP anti-tank gun mounted the German 7.5 cm PaK 40/3 on the Pzkpfw 38(t) chassis.

Flakpanzer 38(t) auf Sf 38(t) Ausf M SP anti-aircraft gun. Yet another conversion of the Pzkpfw 38(t) was this self-propelled anti-aircraft gun, the gun being the 2 cm FlaK38.

Jagdpanzer 38(t) Hetzer tank destroyer. Over 2,500 of these light tank destroyers, the Hetzer (Hunter), were produced, using the basic components of the Pzkpfw 38(t), but with a wider hull. The Swiss Army purchased a number of Hetzers from Czechoslovakia after World War 2.

Bergpanzer 38(t) Hetzer recovery tank (*Below right*). This armoured recovery vehicle was designed to support tank destroyer units armed with Hetzer, upon which it was based, but with an open top and a lower superstructure. It weighed $14\frac{1}{2}$ tons, some $1\frac{1}{4}$ tons lighter than Hetzer.

78

German Medium Tanks

Pzkpfw III Ausf A medium tank The backbone of the German Panzer Divisions were their medium tanks in the 15–20 ton range. The photograph shows one of the early models of the 15-ton Pzkpfw III, the Ausf A. It mounted a 3.7 cm gun, plus twin machine guns in the turret and a third in the hull, manned by the radio operator. Designed in 1935, the first Ausf As were issued in 1937, but withdrawn from service in early 1940 because their armour thickness of only 15 mm was inadequate.

Pzkpfw III Ausf E medium tank. Produced in 1938–39, this was the fifth model of the Pzkpfw III. It still mounted the same armament as the Ausf A, but its armour was now up to 30 mm thick and its weight had gone up to $19\frac{1}{2}$ tons. This version was later rearmed with a 5 cm gun.

Pzkpfw III Ausf F medium tank. Very similar to the Ausf E, the Ausf F started life armed with a 3.7 cm gun, but from the summer of 1940 many were up-gunned by fitting the 5 cm KwK L/42 gun, as seen here.

Pzkpfw III Ausf G medium tank (*Left*).
Six hundred Ausf G model were produced
from April 1940 onwards. The weight was
now just over 20 tons and it mounted a 5 cm
KwK L/42 gun, and had a crew of five.
These tanks were photographed in
Yugoslavia.

Pzkpfw III Ausf F medium tank (*Centre
left*). This was the first model to mount the 5
cm KwK gun and the turret was redesigned
to accept it. First ordered in 1939, it saw
service in the early campaigns in Poland and
France, when it was quickly realised that
more basic armour and bigger guns were
needed. The problem with the Pzkpfw III
was that it could not accept a gun larger
than 5 cm because of the restrictive size of
the turret ring, 4 ins smaller than that of
Pzkpfw IV, which, as will be seen later,
could be fitted with a succession of 75 mm
guns.

Pzkpfw III Ausf L medium tank (*Below*). GIs examine a Pzkpfw III Ausf L,
knocked out during the Kasserine Pass
battle in Tunisia in early 1943. The Ausf L
mounted the 5 cm KwK39 L/60 gun and
once again had thicker armour on the front
of the turret, now 57 mm.

**Panzerbefehlswagen III Tauchfahig
Ausf H submersible command tank**
(*Right*). An excellent shot of a Tauchpanzer
emerging from deep-wading a river during
the early stages of the Russian campaign.
The tank belongs to 18 Panzer Division and
the photograph was probably taken during
the crossing of the River Bug at Patulin in
June 1941.

Pzkpfw III Ausf M medium tank
(*Above*). Side plates and extra armour was
fitted around the turret as protection
against HEAT weapons such as the
Bazooka and PIAT, as seen on this Ausf M,
which also had better fording equipment
than the Ausf L, otherwise they were very
similar. The *Schurzen* (literally 'armoured
skirts') are clearly visible on the tanks of this
Panzer formation as it moves through a
Russian village.

**7.5 cm Sturmgeschutz 40 Ausf assault
gun** (*Below*). The original StuG mounted a
short barrelled 7.5 cm gun on a Pzkpfw III
chassis. Later, the armament was increased
by fitting a long 7.5 cm StuK40. Weighing
just over $21\frac{1}{2}$ tons, with a speed of some 40
km/h, it was also used as a tank destroyer.

7.5 cm StuG Ausf F/8 assault gun/tank destroyer (*Above*). Three StuG are seen here in the Caucasus Mountains in September 1942 during an armed reconnaissance operation.

Pzkpfw IV Ausf B medium tank (*Left*). The best German medium tank was the Pzkpfw IV. It met the requirements for a 20 ton tank, which the Germans had long thought was the ideal size and weight for the main strike weapon of any armoured formation. Early models, such as this Ausf B, mounted a 7.5 cm L/24 low velocity, short barrelled gun. Pzkpfw IV was the only German battle tank to remain in production throughout World War 2.

10.5 cm Sturmhaubitze 42 assault howitzer (*Above*). Designed to provide backup to the more lightly armed StuGs, this 10.5 cm assault howitzer gave the extra punch needed. StuG 42 weighed 24 tons. Over 1,200 were produced between 1942–45.

Pzkpfw IV Ausf D medium tank (*Above right*). Thicker armour on the sides and rear was the main improvement on this model. A hull machine gun, omitted on both the Ausf B and C, was again fitted. Pzkpfw IV was a well made, robust tank with a satisfactory cross country performance and a large turret ring to take more powerful guns.

Pzkpfw IV Ausf E medium tank (*Below*). Extra armour had by now put the weight up to 21 tons, but the main improvement on this particular model was a newly designed commander's cupola. The engine was the Maybach HL120TRM, which gave a top speed of 42 km/h.

Pzkpfw IV Ausf C (*Right*). Dashing young German tank commander stands proudly in the turret of his Panzer IV Ausf C medium tank. He is wearing the very distinctive large floppy black beret (*Schutzmutze*) which had a special padded head protector inside. The short double-breasted jacket and long straight trousers were black also – which helped to hide the inevitable oil stains!

Pzkpfw IV Ausf F$_2$ medium tank (*Top left*). As early as 1941 plans were laid to improve the firepower of Pzkpfw IV by fitting a long barrelled 7.5 cm gun. The Ausf F$_2$ was the first to be so fitted, and stowage arrangements had to be modified to accept the larger rounds. When it first appeared in mid-1942, it was more than a match for any of the contemporary Allied tanks.

Pzkpfw IV Ausf G medium tank (*Below left*). The Ausf G was very like the F$_2$ with minor variations, including thicker side armour. Note the 'Jerricans' on the tank side; these were vastly superior to the far more flimsy British equivalent. This Ausf G was captured in North Africa.

A very different picture (*Below*). A knocked-out Pzkpfw IV Ausf G during the German retreat out of Russia. Now the Allies were able to 'out-*Blitzkrieg*' the Germans.

Sturmpanzer IV assault gun (*Below right*). Known as the Brummbär (Grizzly Bear), this 28-ton assault infantry gun was a formidable weapon, with a 15 cm StuH43 L/12 gun mounted in a box-shaped superstructure on the Pzkpfw IV chassis. Some 300 were built and were first used in the storming of Kursk in 1943.

Pzkpfw IV Ausf H medium tank (*Left*). More of this model were produced than any other. It had better transmission, thicker armour and a new idler. It was the penultimate model in the Pzkpfw IV range. The photograph shows an Ausf G/H found among the ruins in Pontfarcy in the Brest Peninsular in 1944.

Pzkpfw IV Ausf J medium tank (*Above*). Last of the line was the Ausf J, which weighed 25 tons, had a range of over 300 kms and a top speed of 38 km/h. This one has been fitted with *Schurzen* and extra armour round the turret. Its long barrelled 7.5 cm gun had an excellent performance against armour.

Jagdpanzer IV tank destroyer. Sometimes called the Guderian Ente (Guderian Duck), this TD mounted a long barrelled 7.5 cm gun and was first issued in spring 1944. It weighed about 25 tons and had a crew of four. The TD in the photograph has been treated with *Zimmerit*, an anti-magnetic mine paste.

Jagdpanzer IV/70(V) tank destroyer. This was an improved version of the Jagdpanzer IV and mounted the 7.5 cm PaK42 L/70 with an even longer barrel and no muzzle brake. The one shown in this photograph is fitted with armoured side plates (*Schurzen*).

Hornisse 8.8 cm self-propelled heavy anti-tank gun. The Hornisse (Hornet) was also called Nashorn (Rhinoceros). It mounted the 8.8 cm PaK43/1 anti-tank gun on the same chassis as the Hummel (see later). Its combat weight was 24 tons and it had a speed of about 42 km/h. This formidable and highly mobile anti-tank weapon was very effective wherever it was used.

Hummel 15 cm self-propelled heavy howitzer (*Above*). The Hummel (Bumble Bee) mounted a 15 cm howitzer capable of firing a shell weighing nearly 96 lbs to a range of some 14,500 yds. This particular Hummel is seen, complete with camouflage net, on the Russian front.

Möbelwagen 3.7 cm self-propelled anti-aircraft gun (*Below left*). The Möbelwagen (literally 'furniture van') was designed to produce mobile, anti-aircraft gun support to armoured formations. It was only meant as a temporary solution, but mounted a useful 3.7 cm FlaK43 gun with all round traverse – this was still possible at low elevation by dropping the sides of the 'furniture van'.

Wirbelwind 2 cm anti-aircraft tank (*Below right*). The Whirlwind mounted quadruple 2 cm FlaK 38 cannon housed in an armoured roofless turret on the Pzkpfw IV chassis. The AFV was the first German anti-aircraft tank. Production was halted towards the end of 1944, when it was decided to introduce the more effective 3.7 cm FlaK Ostwind.

Ostwind 3.7 cm anti-aircraft tank. The Ostwind (Eastwind) mounted a single 3.7 cm anti-aircraft gun in a six-sided, open topped turret on the converted Pzkpfw IV. By the end of the war 'Ostbau' Sagan had produced only 43, mostly by conversion from gun tanks.

10.5 cm le FH 18/1 (Sf) aus Gesch IVb, SP howitzer. This was a light SP howitzer which mounted a 10.5 cm howitzer on a special chassis which used Pz IV components but was shorter and had a smaller engine. Only eight were built.

Brükenleger IV, tank bridgelayer. Some twenty of these bridgelayers were produced, with two varieties of bridge, the Krupp bridge, as in the photograph, and the Magirus bridge, which had a different method of launch. The bridge span was 9 m.

BW 40 experimental tank. Only one prototype of this experimental model, with a new suspension, was built.

Bergepanzer IV armoured recovery vehicle. From October 1944, a number of Pzkpfw IVs were converted into armoured recovery vehicles by removing the turret and replacing it with a box-body. A derrick crane was also mounted on the rear engine decks.

Experimental 2 cm self-propelled anti-aircraft gun, Möbelwagen. This version of the 'furniture van' did not enter production. It mounted quadruple 2 cm FlaK cannon and had a new, wider superstructure. It was dropped in preference of the 3.7 cm version.

89

German Heavy Tanks

Panther Ausf D. Allied troops investigate a captured Panther Ausf D which has been painted with *Zimmerit* (anti-magnetic mine paste). Its frontal armour was 100 mm thick.

PzkpfwV Ausf D heavy tank. The Germans kept up their superiority tank *versus* tank by bringing into service the Pzkpfw V and VI heavy tanks in the 40–60 ton range, well ahead of the Allies. Pzkpfw V, or Panther as it is more commonly called, owes much of its design to a detailed study undertaken of the Russian T-34 which had been able to deal easily with the Pzkpfw IIIs and IVs. The Ausf D model Panther, seen here during trials in 1943, weighed 43 tons, mounted a 7.5 cm KwK42/L70 gun and had a crew of five. With a top speed of about 45 km/h, and a radius of action of 200 km, Panther was a formidable opponent.

Pzkpfw Ausf D. An excellent photograph of an Ausf D. A total of 850 of this model was built and it was the first to go into service, despite the fact that the model which followed it was called Ausf A!

Pzkpfw V Ausf A heavy tank. The second model of the Panther to be produced was the Ausf A of which some 2,000 were built between August 1943 and May 1944. It had various improvements over the earlier model, including a new commander's cupola and better running gear. Two Ausf As are seen here under attack in Russia.

Panther Ausf A. US soldiers investigate a Panther, partly buried in a bomb crater in Normandy – the result of the terrific Allied aerial bombardment which preceded the American breakout. The Ausf A weighed 44.8 tons and had thicker armour – the front of the turret was now 110 mm thick.

Pzkpfw V Ausf G heavy tank. The Ausf G was produced as a result of combat experience with the Ausf D and A. Over 3,000 Ausf G were built between March 1944 and April 1945. The hull was redesigned, now without the driver's vision visor which must have been a vulnerable spot. Seen here alongside a Tiger, this Panther has clearly suffered damage to its right-hand sprocket. The weight of the Ausf G was $45\frac{1}{2}$ tons.

Panzerbefehlswagen Panther command tank. The command version had an additional radio at the expense of some ammunition stowage. Conversions included both the earlier model Ausf D, seen here, and the Ausf A and G.

Jagdpanther heavy tank destroyer. Of the various special adaptations of Panther, the Jagdpanther, heavy tank destoyer, was perhaps the most famous. It mounted an 8.8 cm PaK 43/3 L/71 gun which could penetrate 182 mm of armour at 500 m. It was a well protected, fast (46 km/h) and effective tank destroyer.

Bergepanther armoured recovery vehicle. This was the ARV version of the Panther, designed to deal with the recovery of heavy tanks. Some were factory built and others converted from gun tanks, the aim being to provide a turretless tank, complete with winch, spade anchor and derrick. This Bergepanther was abandoned near Bastogne after the Battle of the Bulge.

All round views of Pzkpfw VI Tiger heavy tank. The most famous of all German tanks was the Tiger, although only 1,354 were ever produced as compared with some 6,000 Panthers. Tiger production began in July 1942 and the first saw action in Russia in August 1942. Weighing some 57 tons, Tiger's main armament was the dreaded 8.8 cm KwK36 L/56 gun that could penetrate 112 mm of armour at 500 m. To the average Allied soldier, the Tiger became the symbol of the invincibility of German armour, to a degree which completely outweighed its true capabilities, although, when it was introduced, it was undoubtedly the most powerful tank in the world. It was not really matched by the Allies until the introduction of the Pershing with its 90 mm gun, some three years later (March 1945), which emphasises the considerable German lead in tank design. But Tiger did have its weak points, one of them being its very low geared turret traverse, which made bringing the main gun to bear on a target very slow, thus enabling Allied tanks to get in their shots first. The tank was also very heavy and had both a limited top speed of 38 km/h and range of 100–140 kms.

93

Tiger, wading equipment. British troops are seen here examining sections of a snorkel tube which could be fitted to the Tiger for deep wading. With the tank properly sealed and the tube in place, Tiger could wade to a depth of about 12–13 ft.

Tiger, internal views. These three photographs show the interior of a Tiger driving compartment and two views of the turret.

Tiger Mörser assault howitzer (*Near right*). The 38 cm heavy mortar version of the Tiger was designed for use against heavy fortifications and fired a rocket-assisted projectile. It was very heavy – 65 tons. Here, a British crewed ARV pass a Tiger Mörser that was knocked out by the US 9th Army.

Ferdinand tank destroyer (*Far right*). Also called 'Elefant', this 65-ton tank destroyer/heavy assault gun, mounted a 8.8 cm StuK 43/2 L/71 gun in a limited traverse mount. Ferdinand was ideal when used as a long range tank killer, but not nearly as effective as an assault gun because of its lack of traverse and the absence of any close-in defensive capability. The latter problem was solved by fitting an MG34, but Elefant was really only at its best when fighting at long range – it is reputed to have knocked out a T-34 at three miles range!

Pzkpfw VI Ausf B heavy tank. The Königstiger (Royal or King Tiger) or Tiger 2, as it was called, was a formidable heavy tank that could deal with any of its opponents on the battlefield with ease. It weighed over 68 tons, was armed with a long barrelled 8.8 cm KsK43 L/71 gun which could penetrate 182 mm of armour at 500 m. It was thus able to deal effortlessly with the heaviest Allied tanks. However, its sheer weight and bulk gave it a relatively poor cross country performance and made for problems in maintenance and reliability. Only 489 King Tigers were built (between January 1944 and March 1945) and they were used mainly in the defensive battles as the Allies pressed deep into Germany.

Tiger P heavy tank (*Near right*). Only five Tiger Ps were ever built during July 1942 by Porsche. It had a different suspension and power train, two V-10 air-cooled engines instead of the single Maybach water-cooled engine.

Pzkpfw Maus – super heavy tank (*Far right*). The heaviest tank *ever* built, Maus weighed in at an incredible 188 tons. Only two prototypes were built, although others were started but never completed. Only one Maus, seen here, had a turret and armament, one 12.8 cm L/55 gun and one coaxial 7.5 cm L/36.5 gun, fitted. Both were destroyed by the Germans.

Jagdtiger heavy tank destroyer. This 70-ton monster mounted a 128 mm PaK 80 L/55 gun and was undoubtedly the largest and most powerful armoured fighting vehicle to see combat service in World War 2. Its gun could outrange any other tank gun and could easily penetrate any other tank. The 77 Jagdtigers built saw service in the Ardennes and later in the defence of Germany.

Miscellaneous German Photographs

Driver training (*Left*). A young tank driver receives instruction on how to drive a Pzkpfw 1 Ausf B, which has been specially modified for use at a driver training school.

Naval combat! (*Above*). If the original caption with this photograph can be believed, the sign on the turret represents an enemy destroyer, sunk near Boulogne in 1940.

Bullseye! Even the *Schurzen* on this StuG has had little effect in stopping a direct hit. Credit for this 'kill' went to 4th Armored Division of General Patton's US Third Army near Bitberg, Germany in March 1945.

Tank sledge. One possible way to move infantry across bullet-swept ground when no armoured personnel carriers are available is this large sledge – it must have been both dangerous and uncomfortable!

Wooden tank. GIs inspect a wooden tank: was this a prototype or just a decoy?

Neubaufahrzeug medium tank (*Left*). Only three of these $23\frac{1}{2}$-ton medium tanks were built, after two prototypes were produced in 1934, when the German Army wanted to gain experience with multi-turreted tanks. These three, seen here in Southern Norway, were shipped to Oslo in April 1940 and saw action there.

World War Two

5 Great Britain and the Commonwealth

In the early stages of World War 2, the British continued in much the same haphazard way as they had done during the interwar years, producing obsolete designs, undergunned and lacking in armoured protection. Although these early British tanks proved adequate against even worse Italian and Japanese models, they were markedly inferior to the German panzers. The British were hidebound in having the 2-pdr as their main tank gun and by building tanks with turret rings which were too small to accept anything larger. Consequently, although it had a reasonable AP performance, the 2-pdr was far too small to produce an effective HE round. Dual capability and larger calibre tank guns did not start to appear in the British Army until they began to receive American Grants and Shermans, on Lend-Lease.

The role of light tanks was taken over almost completely by armoured cars. Although the British produced another light model, it was only of use in airborne operations and even then saw little action. The Cruiser range continued through a series of disasters with the odd bright spot here and there, such as Crusader and Cromwell, but generally they were a disappointing bunch with insufficient firepower and protection, together with poor mechanical reliability despite their speed. Probably the most successful line was that of the Infantry tank, starting with the Matilda. Valentine and then Churchill both proved their worth, despite an initial lack of firepower. However, they were adequately protected and that meant a good deal to the crews who had to man them against enemy tanks armed with larger calibre, more powerful guns.

Despite the fact that British tank production was, in numbers, on a par with that of Germany, the British still needed American tanks, such as the ubiquitous Sherman, to equip many of their armoured formations. The British also produced the most effective Sherman of the war, the Sherman Firefly, by mounting on it their very effective 17-pdr gun.

Apart from the building of the Ram in Canada, together with large numbers of Valentines for Russia, the Commonwealth had little effect, if any, upon tank design and production during the war. They relied heavily on Britain and America to produce the tanks with which to equip their armoured formations.

The last British tank to enter operational service in World War 2 was undoubtedly the best of all, namely the Comet. Its successor, the even better Centurion, was the beginning of a period of highly successful British tank design which is still continuing with Chieftain and Challenger. However, during the majority of the war, British tanks were outgunned consistently by the Germans. It was only a total air superiority, plus the sheer weight of numbers, which the Allies enjoyed from Normandy onwards, that eventually tipped the scales in their favour.

A13 Mark III Cruiser tank Mark V. Known as the Covenanter, this followed the Mk IVA Cruiser. It weighed some 4 tons more, at 18 tons, and had armour up to 40 mm thick. It was also lower than the Mark IV Cruiser by some 14 ins, and was powered by a 280 hp Meadows engine. Covenanter never saw action. It was used mainly in the training role in the UK although a few were sent to the Middle East where they were used for training. This photograph shows a Covenanter on a recruiting parade in Perth in 1941.

British Light Tanks

Harry Hopkins light tank Mark VIII. Last of the line of light tanks was the 8½-ton Harry Hopkins. Like the Tetrach which it was designed to replace, its recce role was taken over by the armoured car. Harry Hopkins was never used in the airborne role, as was Tetrach, and the 100 or so Mark VIIIs built did not even enter service.

Alecto dozer. A self-propelled howitzer, the 95 mm Alecto, was designed using the Harry Hopkins chassis; another version mounted a 6-pdr. A small number of dozers were also completed late in the war, with a dozer blade replacing the gun. None of these AFVs saw operational service.

British Cruiser Tanks

A10 Cruiser tank Mark II (*Below left*). Designed as the successor to the A9 Cruiser (see earlier section 'Between the Wars'), production started in 1938 of this 13¾-ton heavy cruiser tank, which entered service in 1939. The A10 saw service in both France and the Western Desert, it had a 2-pdr (or 3.7 in howitzer in the close support version) as its main armament, plus two Besa machine guns. The maximum armour thickness was 30 mm.

A13 Cruiser tank Mark III (*Below*). This was the first cruiser to have the Christie suspension and was designed as a high speed replacement for the A9 and A10. It entered service in 1939 and saw service in France and the Western Desert. Weighing 14 tons, the four-man A13 had a top speed of 30 mph and a range of about 90 miles. Armour was only 14 mm thick, under half that of the A10.

A13 Mark II Cruiser tank Mark IV (*Left*). This was the up-armoured version of the A13, with armour now up to 30 mm thick. Note the 'V' shaped sides which have been added to the turret. These were hollow in fact, thus giving spaced armour to protect against hollow charge weapons. The extra armour added about ¾ ton on to the tank, but this did not materially affect its performance, as the Nuffield V-12 engine had plenty of power available.

A13 Mark II Cruiser tank Mark IVA (*Below*). Later production models had an armour cover on the gun mantlet and the co-ax machine gun was now a Besa instead of a Vickers.

Covenanter IV (*Above*). The production model of the Covenanter IV had a different mantlet, as seen here, to the pilots models, and various Marks incorporated a number of improvements. The Mark IV, seen here, had a better engine cooling system to try to rectify the overheating problems which plagued the Covenanter, but they were never satisfactorily overcome.

Covenanter CS (*Left*). The Close-Support version was armed with a 3 in howitzer in place of the normal 2-pdr. This photograph shows a Covenanter III CS on training in UK.

Covenanter with AMRA (*Below*). The Anti-Mine Roller Attachment was tried out on a Covenanter in 1942. The device was pushed in front of the tank in order to set-off mines by pressure.

Covenanter Bridgelayer. A 30 ft scissors-type bridge was designed in the mid-1930s for use on both cruiser and infantry tanks (see Matilda bridgelayer later). Some Covenanters were fitted and a few actually saw service with the Australians in Burma in 1942.

Crusader Mark III (*Below*). The final production model mounted a 6-pdr gun instead of the original 2-pdr, plus slightly thicker armour. Note also the armoured 'skirts'.

A15 Cruiser tank Mark VI Crusader (*Above left*). The Crusader was undoubtedly the best of the early Cruisers, and a total 5,300 Crusaders was built, the first entering service in 1941. Heavier than Covenanter, Crusader still had a high top speed, 27 mph, and its cross country performance was good. It did, however, lack protection and was easy meat for contemporary German anti-tank and tank guns. The photograph shows the Mark II Crusader.

Crusader in disguise. This Crusader, being loaded onto a tank transporter, has been disguised to look like a lorry. Note the extra fuel tank on the rear, which gave the tank an extra 27 miles range.

Crusader II AA Mark I. A single Bofors 40 mm anti-aircraft gun was mounted in an open-topped shield in place of the normal turret.

Crusader III AA Mark II (*Right*). A far better conversion than the Mark I, the Mark II had a twin 20 mm Oerlikon anti-aircraft mounted in a properly designed turret. A similar mount was also fitted to the Centaur tank, but with Polsten instead of Oerlikon cannons.

A27L Cruiser tank Mark VIII Centaur. Next in the Cruiser line was Centaur. It had been intended to fit the tank with a new engine, the Rolls-Royce Meteor. However, supplies were not available because all production was required for aircraft. Consequently the old Liberty V-12 engine was fitted instead, as it was decided to keep the Meteor engine for the next in line, Cromwell.

A24 Cruiser tank Mark VII Cavalier. Experience with Crusader and its predecessors led to the production of the first new wartime Cruiser, the Cavalier, which had thicker armour (up to 76 mm), a bigger gun, the 6-pdr, and wider tracks. All this increased its weight by an extra 5 tons over Crusader, and its top speed was lower, as it used the same engine and power train. Cavalier was only built in small numbers and was never used operationally as a gun tank, although some were converted for artillery OP use.

Centaur dozer. Nearly 1,000 Centaurs were completed. A proportion of these were later converted to Cromwell by the installation of the Merlin engine, and others were converted to specialised roles, such as this dozer. The turret was removed and a winch and jib fitted to operate the dozer blade. It was issued on a scale of one per squadron. This dozer, belonging to the 7th Armoured Division, was in fact photographed after the war giving a demonstration to Dutch soldiers.

Centaur ARV. Again minus turret, with a winch fitted into the space thus vacated. The armoured recovery vehicle was used by squadron fitters and had a dismountable A-frame jib.

A27M Cruiser tank Mark VIII Cromwell. Early Cromwells closely resembled the Cavalier and Centaur, except, of course, for the fitting of the Meteor engine – hence the letter 'M'. The Meteor engine was a 600 hp V-12 and made Cromwell the fastest Cruiser tank so far, with increased reliability. Cromwell became the most important British built Cruiser tank of World War 2, and formed the main equipment of British armoured divisions in 1944–45, together with the American built Sherman M4 (see later). Undoubtedly there were misgivings among some when converted from Sherman to Cromwell (*e.g.* 7th Armoured Division was re-equipped when they returned to the UK from Italy to prepare for D-Day), because of its lack of firepower – it was armed with either a 75 mm or a 6-pdr gun, neither of which was a real match for Tiger or Panther. The photograph is of a column of Cromwells training in the UK. The column is led by a Cromwell VI, the Close Support version which mounted the 95 mm howitzer. It was followed by 75 mm gun tanks (Mark IV onwards).

Cromwell Mark III (*Left*). In 1943, the remaining Centaurs were converted into Cromwells by the installation of the Meteor engine. The re-engined Centaur, initially called Cromwell X, retained the 6-pdr gun.

Cromwell Mark IV (*Centre left*). Similarly, the Centaur III was re-engined with the new Meteor engine and was known as the Cromwell IV. Its armament was the 75 mm gun.

A30 Cruiser tank – Challenger. The main drawback to Cromwell was its lack of gun power, so it was logical to produce a tank with more hitting power to back up the 75 mm gun, so Challenger was designed to mount the British 17-pdr gun (*c.f.* Sherman Firefly). This required a larger turret and led to the need to increase both the length and width of the hull. A sixth road wheel was introduced and the all up weight increased to 32 tons. Production of Challenger was much slower than Sherman Firefly, by September 1944, there were only enough to provide three armoured regiments with twelve each.

Cromwell with CIRD (*Below right*). The Canadian Indestructible Roller Device was designed to explode mines and thus gap a minefield. Although this was issued to units it was never used operationally.

A30 self-propelled gun – Avenger (*Right*). This was a British attempt to produce a tank destroyer, armed with a 17-pdr gun, with an open-topped turret in order to reduce weight. Avenger was a stop-gap weapon whilst the Valentine Archer SP was being put into production and before the British began to get supplies of the American M10. Avenger was not ready in time to be used operationally and by the time the pilot model was completed it had been decided to switch production effort to Comet.

A34 Cruiser tank Comet, pilot model (*Below*). The next logical development of the Centaur/Cromwell design was to produce a tank that really had the firepower, protection and mobility to match its German counterparts. It mounted a completely redesigned gun, a 76.2 mm (3 in), known as the 77 mm, which had just about the same performance as the 17-pdr, but was smaller and lighter. The initial Comet prototype, seen here, used the Cromwell suspension without top rollers.

A41 Medium gun tank – Centurion (*Above right*). Although the Centurion development began in 1943, it did not reach troop trials stage until May 1945, so was never used in action in World War 2. The Mark I had a crew of four, weighed 48 tons and was armed with a 17-pdr gun plus a Polsten 20 mm cannon as co-ax (after the first 10 pilots, this was changed to a Besa machine gun). The Centurion went on to be upgunned first to a 20-pdr, then to 105 mm and was produced in many different Marks over its highly successful lifespan with the British Army. It is still in service with other nations all over the world.

A34 Cruiser tank – Comet. The best all round British tank produced during World War 2, Comet weighed 32¾ tons, had a crew of five and was armed with two machine guns, one in the hull, as well as its 77 mm main armament. It had a good cross country performance, a top speed of 32 mph and armour up to 102 mm thick. It was the last British cruiser to have the Christie suspension. Sadly, Comet was introduced too late to have much effect on tank *versus* tank combat in World War 2. However, it remained in service for the next fifteen years, the last Comets not being withdrawn from British service until 1960. Its successor was the A41 Centurion.

British Infantry Tanks

Matilda Close Support (*Above*). The CS version mounted a 3 in howitzer in place of the 2-pdr; note also the Bren gun on an AA mounting of this Matilda CS photographed during a Royal Review in UK in 1941.

A12 Infantry tank Mark II, Matilda II (*Left*). Although the Matilda II was designed in 1937, it did not properly enter service until after the war had started, there being only two A12s in service when war was declared. A few more were issued to 7th Royal Tank Regiment in 1940 and were used to great effect in the Arras counter-attack just prior to Dunkirk. However, it was in the early desert battles against the Italians, that Matilda reigned supreme. Its 2-pdr gun, thick armour (up to 78 mm) and reasonable cross country performance, made it a firm favourite with tank crews. The photograph shows an early model which had a Vickers as its co-axial machine gun.

Matilda Dozer (*Right*). This was an Australian adaptation of the gun tank, with the addition of a box-like dozer blade. The dozer here was in action in New Guinea.

A12 Infantry tank Mark IIA, Matilda III (*Left*). Nearly 3,000 Matildas were produced in all. The photograph shows the Matilda III which had twin Leyland engines to replace the twin AEC of the earlier models. It also had a Besa machine gun instead of the Vickers. Top speed of the Matilda was 15 mph, but cross country only about 8 mph. Here, sheltering beside a battered building at El Adem in 1942, a Matilda and its crew take a well-earned break.

Matilda Baron – mine clearing tank (*Right*). Various types of mine clearing devices were tried on Matilda, such as the Baron chain flail, seen here, which cleared a lane through a minefield by beating the ground with flails to set-off any mines in its path. The photograph shows the last Baron, the Mark IIIA, on which the turret and main armament had been removed to save weight. However, it was only used for training because of the production of the Sherman Crab (see later).

Matilda Frog flamethrowing tank.
Another Australian adaptation was the fitting of a flamethrower in a tube, to replace the 2-pdr. Fuel for the flame-gun was carried in the turret. Matilda Frog was used successfully in New Guinea.

Infantry tank Mark III – Valentine. The prototype of the Valentine was produced by Vickers on 14 February 1940, hence its name. Over 8,000 Valentines were built, and the tank remained in production until 1944. It was also built in Canada (see later). Initial models were armed with 2-pdr guns, as seen here, plus a co-axial machine gun.

Infantry tank Mark III – Valentine XI. The Valentine had a variety of main armaments, the 2-pdr giving way to the 6-pdr and then to the 75 mm as seen here on what was the final model. It was of welded rather than rivetted construction.

Infantry tank Mark III – Valentine. A British armoured division, equipped with Valentines, is lined up on parade for an inspection by His Majesty The King, 12 September 1941.

Valentine bridgelayer. A 30 ft scissors-type bridge was carried on the Valentine, the class 30 bridge and hydraulic equipment taking the place of the turret. Although a few were used in Burma, the majority did not see operational service.

Valentine flamethrower. A variety of flamethrowing equipment was tried on Valentine, this one being gas-operated. It was from tests with this equipment that the Crocodile equipment was developed, which was used successfully on the Churchill tank (see later).

Self-propelled Gun – Bishop (*Left*). The successful use by the Germans of self-propelled guns on various tank chassis in North Africa, gave rise to an urgent request from the Eighth Army for similar weapons. The first was Bishop, which comprised a 25-pdr gun mounted in a box-like turret on a Valentine tank chassis. After 1943, it was mostly relegated to the training role and its place taken by the much better designed Priest (see later).

Self-propelled Gun – Archer (*Left*). Another use for the extremely lethal 17-pdr gun was as a tank destroyer. Archer reached production by March 1944. It was used to equip divisional anti-tank battalions from October 1944 onwards and remained in service for about ten years after the end of the war. This low, open-topped SP, which had a top speed of about 15 mph, carried 39 rounds.

A22 Infantry tank Mark IV – Churchill (*Left*). This was the first British tank to be completely designed during World War 2 and it remained in production throughout the entire war. The earliest model, produced in 1941, weighed 38½ tons and was armed with a 2-pdr gun in the turret and a 3 in Close-Support howitzer in its nose, alongside the driver. With armour up to 102 mm thick, a good cross country performance, albeit on the slow side, the Churchill was perhaps the best and most well liked British tank of the war. Churchills first saw action during the disastrous Dieppe raid of August 1942.

Churchill IV (NA75) (*Right*). This was the very first British tank to mount a 75 mm gun, the guns and mantlets being salvaged from knocked out Shermans in Tunisia. They were used with great success in Sicily and Italy, this particular Churchill being photographed in the narrow streets of Montefiore.

Mr Winston Churchill (*Above*). As usual, 'Winnie' is smoking a cigar, as he steps into the first production Churchill, to which he had given his name, in June 1941.

Churchill II (*Right*). It was rapidly decided to dispense with the nose 3 in the howitzer and replace it with a Besa machine gun, as seen on this Churchill II leaving a tank landing craft.

Churchill VI. From the Mark III onwards, Churchill mounted a 6-pdr gun in the turret, but this was later replaced by a 75 mm, as seen here, as the tank ploughs through a muddy stream in Germany on its way into the Reichwald Forest.

Churchill VII. The weight of the Churchill had now risen to 40 tons, with a welded/cast turret and 75 mm gun. Note also that the escape doors are round instead of square. This model was used in North West Europe for many years after the war.

Churchill VIII. The Close-Support version of the Mark VII, the Mark VIII mounted a 95 mm howitzer as its main armament. The other CS version was Churchill V which had a 95 mm instead of the 6-pdr.

Churchill X LT. Various early marks were reworked and had applique armour fitted on nose and sides. The photograph shows a reworked Mark VI, which retained the original lighter turret – hence the initials LT.

British tanks for Russia. Troops load a tank train with Matildas, Valentines and Churchills, destined for Russia.

Churchill 3 in Gun Carrier. An early wartime requirement was to produce a tank carrying a high velocity gun of large calibre. This version mounted a 3 in anti-aircraft gun in a mount with limited traverse. A small number were produced but they did not see operational service.

Churchill ARV (*Left*). Two versions of the armoured recovery vehicle were produced on the Churchill chassis. The first had the turret removed, while the later ARV Mark II had a wooden box-shaped dummy turret (seen here) with jibs front and rear and a 25-ton two speed winch.

Churchill Bridgelayer (*Below*). The original caption to this photograph of a Churchill bridgelayer with its 30 ft bridge in the travelling position, explains that its nickname was 'London Bridge'!

Churchill Ark (*Left*). Various types of bridge were designed for carriage on the Churchill chassis, one of the first being the Churchill Ark. There were different patterns (UK and Italian) and they were used to great effect. The photograph shows two Arks, one on top of the other, being used to span the Senio River in Italy.

Churchill Arks (*Bottom left*). Two Italian pattern Arks moving up. The major difference to the UK pattern was the absence of trackway on the hull top, the actual tank tracks acting as trackways.

Churchill Great Eastern Ramp (*Below*). Weighing 46 tons, the Great Eastern Ramp resembled the Ark but had a much more elevated and heavier trackway. The front 25-ft ramps were fired into position by rockets. The rocket magazine was at the rear.

Extra armour (*Right*). Track plates are festooned around the turret of this Churchill belonging to the Guards Armoured Division, while US Airborne troops cluster on top. They are in the village of Appelhausen, a few miles from Munster, in April 1945.

Churchill Ark UK Pattern (*Above*). Interesting view of the front of an Ark in a ditch while a tank crosses.

Churchill with Farmer plough (*Right*). One method of removing mines was to plough them up and this photograph shows one type of plough used. In fact there were three varieties of Farmer plough: Farmer Front, Farmer Deck and, seen here, Farmer Track. None were used operationally.

Churchill with CIRD. The Canadian indestructible roller device was produced by the Canadians in 1943. Two arms were fixed to the front of the tank, each supporting a heavy roller. When the roller detonated a mine it was saved from damage because of its flexible mounting which enabled it to rotate around the arm.

Close-up of AVRE mortar. The Spigot mortar on the Churchill AVRE was of 290 mm calibre and proved an ideal demolition weapon. As can be seen, it bolted on to the 6-pdr mount.

Churchill AVRE with twin Bobbins. One of the various mat-laying devices which were fitted to Churchill was this twin bobbin which had two small bobbins of hessian and chespaling, suitable for heavy vehicles. Seen here on trial, leaving an LCT.

Churchill AVRE with fascine. Oldest method of filling a ditch was with a large bundle of brushwood, some 6–8 ft in diameter and 11 ft long. These were carried on the front of the tank on a cradle and could be jettisoned by a quick release mechanism from inside.

Churchill AVRE with Bobbin Mark II. The mat laid was 9 ft 11 in wide. The AVRE seen here laying its matting was on trial at Brancaster beach in Norfolk, which was similar to the Normandy beaches as it contained strips of blue clay where AFVs could easily get bogged – hence the need for matting. These mats were developed by 79th Armoured Division and were used during the Normandy landings.

Churchill Oke (*Above*). This was an early form of flamethrowing tank, developed in 1942. Three Okes went on the Dieppe raid in August 1942 but all were destroyed before they could use their flame projectors, which had a range of 40–50 yds.

Churchill Crocodile (*Right*). Some 800 Crocodiles were produced during the war and proved a most effective weapon, continuing in service right up to the Korean war. The trailer carried the flame fluid and there was sufficient for 80 one-second bursts, over a range of 80–120 yds. The Churchill Mark VII was adapted to the Crocodile role, the flame-gun replacing the hull mounted machine gun, so the tank's main armament could still be used.

Ardeer Aggie (*Below*). This strange weapon was specifically designed to improve the power of the AVRE mortar. It was recoilless, the discharge of the main projectile being balanced by firing a dummy projectile rearwards! Trials showed it to be impractible.

Churchill with Jones Onion. One of a number of charge placing devices mounted on Churchill to breach or demolish obstacles. 1,000 lb HE charges were fixed to a frame attached to the front and kept upright by two arms. On reaching the obstacle, the frame was released and a pair of legs at the bottom of the frame met the ground first and made sure that it fell forwards and not back against the tank! The tank reversed away. The explosives were set-off remotely.

A43 Infantry tank Black Prince. Basically a Churchill VII, but with a wider hull and larger turret containing a 17-pdr gun. Trials prototypes were delivered in May 1945, too late for the European war. No production order followed testing as the A41 Centurion was a much better tank. Known originally as 'Super Churchill', it weighed 50 tons, had a crew of five and 6 in thick armour on the turret front but was underpowered, only managing a top road speed of $10\frac{1}{2}$ mph.

5 WORLD WAR TWO GREAT BRITAIN AND THE COMMONWEALTH

British Heavy Tanks

TOG 1 heavy tank. The initials 'TOG' stand for 'The Old Gang', which refers to a team set up on the outbreak of war to find solutions to UK tank needs. The members were all men who had been directly responsible for the very successful World War 1 tank programme – Stern, Wilson, Swinton, d'Eyncourt, Ricardo, Symes and Tritton. They produced a very large, heavy tank – weighing some 80 tons, which was long enough to cross wide trenches and was well protected against anti-tank weapons. It would probably have been ideal to fight the kind of battles of World War 1, but it was entirely wrong for World War 2. It was designed to have a crew of eight, a top speed of 5–8 mph and a range of about 80 miles. It had a 75 mm howitzer in its nose and a 2-pdr in a Matilda II turret on top.

TOG 2 – heavy tank. The trials of TOG 1 showed that there were problems with the electric transmission and so an hydraulic transmission was tried out on TOG 2, which also mounted a larger turret and a 6-pdr gun (later changed to a 17-pdr). A lighter version of TOG was planned but it was not built and the project was shelved in 1944. Only TOG 2 remains (at Bovington Tank Museum), the heaviest British tank of World War 2.

A33 – heavy assault tank. In late 1942, it was proposed that instead of both the infantry tank (Churchill) and the cruiser tank (Cromwell), it would be much better to concentrate on just one type of universal tank that could perform both roles and much else besides. Various designs were tried but only the A33 reached pilot model stage. At 40-tons, this was in essence a Cromwell hull and turret, but with added armour, having a maximum thickness of 114 mm (38 mm thicker than a standard Cromwell), and mounted on the tracks and suspension of the American M6 heavy tank (see later section). A second pilot had a suspension designed in the UK, using vertical coil springs and widened Cromwell tracks. By later 1943 it was clear that the Churchill was well worth continued production, so the A33 project was dropped. Sometimes called 'Excelsior', the one remaining A33 (with M6 suspension) is on show at Bovington.

A38 Valiant – infantry tank (*Above*). Designed as a successor to the Valentine, this small 27-tonner was some 10 tons heavier than its predecessor. Design began in 1943, two pilot models were built, one with a GMC 210 hp engine and AEC gearbox, the other with a Rolls-Royce 350 hp engine and gearbox. One had a 6-pdr gun, the other a 75 mm. Only the GMC version with its 75 mm gun remains – again on show at the Tank Museum.

A39 Tortoise. Last of this odd quintet was the British equivalent of the Jagdtiger, a 75 ton monster, appropriately called Tortoise, which was armed with a 32-pdr gun with limited traverse, had armour up to 228 mm thick and a crew of seven. Although it was first projected in 1942, work progressed slowly until 1944, when the Jagdtiger appeared and the project received extra impetus. However, the six pilot models were not delivered until after the war had ended. Troop trials were carried out in Germany in 1948 and the tanks each covered 100 miles on their tracks plus some 650 miles on transporters. The tanks performance and manoeuverability were adequate, with a top speed 12 mph, but it was really too heavy to be a feasible proposition. The only remaining model is at the Tank Museum.

Commonwealth Tanks

Australia: AC1 – Sentinel cruiser tank. In late 1940 it was decided to design a tank which could be produced in Australia, using easily obtainable items, such as truck engines. The Sentinel, as the result was called, was initially produced in two versions, the first of these being the AC1. This mounted a 2-pdr gun, plus two Vickers machine guns. The cast hull and turret were mounted on a suspension which resembled the French Hotchkiss design, while various parts were copied from the American M3 medium tank (*e.g.* the final drives and transmission). One of the most striking features was the very large sleeve for the bow machine gun. Production began in 1942 and some 60 plus tanks were made, but these were only used for training.

Australia: AC3 – Sentinel cruiser tank. The second Sentinel model, AC2, was not proceeded with, so the next Sentinel to reach prototype stage was AC3, which mounted a 25-pdr in a larger turret. The triple engines (three Cadillac V-8s) were now given a single crankcase. The AC3 did not get further than testing.

Australia: AC4 – Sentinel cruiser tank. The next Sentinel model to be produced mounted a 17-pdr and this prototype was completed in 1943, but no further AC production followed.

Australia: AC3 Test vehicle with twin guns. In order to try out the feasibility of mounting such a powerful gun as the 17-pdr, and before one could be obtained from UK, twin 25-pdrs were tried in a co-axial mount as seen here, in order to simulate this extra recoil, greater in fact than that of the 17-pdr. The trial was a success, but went no further.

Canada: Ram – Mark I cruiser tank. In early 1941 it was decided to produce a tank in Canada based largely on the US M3 medium but better suited to Canadian needs. It was to have a Canadian-produced turret and main armament, together with a redesigned hull to avoid the excessively tall silhouette of the M3. The Ram 1 went into production in late 1941. It mounted a 2-pdr gun.

Canada: Ram Mark II cruiser tank. After only 50 Ram 1s had been produced the main armament was changed to a 6-pdr, equipped with stabilisation. A further 1,000 plus were produced and used for training in Canada and UK. The only Rams to see action were those converted to APCs (known as Ram Kangaroos). The coming of the US Sherman M4 made the Ram unnecessary as the new tank incorporated most of the features which had been found lacking in the M3. Canada did go on to build their own version of the Sherman M4A1, known as the Grizzly, which had certain minor alterations to make it more suitable for UK and Canadian use.

Canada: Skink anti-aircraft tank. One variation of the Gizzly was the Skink. This mounted four 20 mm Polsten cannon. Skink was approved for full production. However, following the realisation that the Allies had virtually total air superiority in Europe, the requirement for AA protection lessened, and production was cancelled.

Canada: Sexton self-propelled gun. The Ram chassis was also used as the basis for the Sexton self-propelled gun which mounted a 25-pdr howitzer and was the British equivalent of the American M7 HMC, which was known as Priest in the British Army. The M7 used the chassis of the M3 medium tank (see later), one of the basic differences being that the driver sat on the opposite side to the Ram. The Priest was issued to British units initially, but was phased out as the Sexton became available. The Sexton had a crew of six (commander, driver, gunner, gunlayer and loader, plus a wireless operator), and stowage for 105 rounds of 25-pdr ammunition, including a proportion of AP.

Canada: Canadian-built Valentine. As we have already seen Australian adaptations of British tanks such as Matilda, it is worth showing one of the 1,420 Valentines that were built in Canada at the Canadian Pacific Montreal Loco Works. The vast majority were shipped to Russia under Lend-Lease.

Canada: American Ford 6-ton tanks on their way to Canada (*Above*). To assist the Canadians in training in the early days of the war, the USA sent all their old Heavy Tank Mark VIIIs and Ford 6-tonners. All were sold virtually at scrap value, and were used for training until more modern tanks became available. Here a trainload of Ford 6-tonners arrives at Camp Borden.

New Zealand: Bob Semple tank (*Top right*). Only four of these armoured agricultural tractors were built in 1940–41, and named after the New Zealand Defence Minister. At 20–25 tons with a box-like body, it was soon found to be impracticable and the idea was dropped.

New Zealand: Schofield Wheel and Track light tank (*Centre and bottom right*). This tank was built in prototype form only during the dark days of 1940, when it was clear that Britain could not produce enough tanks for its own forces, let alone the Commonwealth. It had a cylindrical turret mounting a 2-pdr gun and its ingenious suspension had both wheels and tracks. As the photograph shows, it would run on either, achieving about 26 mph on tracks and 46 mph on wheels. It was not proceeded with further.

World War Two

6 Russia

The Russians took little interest in tanks and tank design during World War 1. A few British and French tanks were left in Russia after the Revolution, bought by the Imperial Government and then captured by the Bolsheviks. These formed the basis of their emerging tank forces, the Renault for instance, being copied and built locally as the 'Russky-Renault'. Other foreign designs were similarly copied, but there were no worthwhile tank formations in the Red Army in the 1920s. Sustained Russian interest in armour did not commence until the start of the First Five Year Plan which included the intended mechanisation of their forces. By 1927, the position had vastly improved, factories had been built and a test and training organisation established. It is interesting to see that they chose to help the Germans at this time by clandestinely allowing them to use the Kazan testing establishment, in defiance of the Versailles Treaty.

By the early 1930s, Russia had followed much the same pattern as everyone else, with two main opposing schools of thought – the one, that tanks should be subordinate to infantry, the other, that they should take over the cavalry role. Russian tanks saw action in Spain and their tank forces grew enormously, until, by the mid-1930s, they had the largest tank force in the world, albeit one of doubtful quality. This was proved by the ease with which the invading Germans dealt with them in the early days of operation *Barbarossa*, knocking out over 17,000 tanks in the first six months. However, there was one bright spot on the Russian horizon. In 1930, they had acquired the rights to manufac-ture the Christie tank, designed by that brilliant but irascible American tank designer, Walter J. Christie. His suspension was used as the basis for a completely new design, the BT-1 medium tank. From this line of mediums was developed one of the most successful tanks the world has ever seen, the T34. The Germans did not meet with the new tank in any significant numbers until the autumn of 1941. Its shock effect was then tremendous and caused the Germans to completely rethink their own tank designs. For their part, the Russians went from strength to strength. They dispensed with the light tank, appreciating that it could never mount heavy enough guns. Instead they geared their enormous manufacturing potential to the production of medium and heavy tanks, which they produced in great numbers. These were supplemented by further generous supplies of tanks from their major Allies, the Americans and British.

The secret of Russian tank design and production was simplicity. They built robust, well shaped and well armed tanks, but without any of the frills and built-in crew comforts that other tank producing countries considered essential. So there were no turret baskets, only simple sighting and firing gear, the maximum number of common components between types, and rough external finish where it did not matter. All this added up to the successful mass production of an enormous tank force which swamped Germany and has now dominated the post-war world with its size and power.

SU76 self-propelled gun. The T70 was used as the basis for the 76.2 mm anti-tank gun. The driver, engines and fuel tanks were all moved to the front so that the gun could be mounted on the rear in a box-shaped hull. The gun had a range of over 12,000 yds, but, when using armoured piercing ammunition, its effective range was greatly reduced – ideal engagement ranges were around 500 m. As soon as the Germans started to up-armour their tanks, the SU76 was relegated to the infantry support role.

Russian Light Tanks

T26 light tank crew. The commander of a Russian T26 light tank unit briefs his tank commanders. They wear an interesting collection of headgear, including the familiar padded tank helmet. This photograph was taken in July 1941, only a few weeks after the Germans had launched their invasion, Operation 'Barbarossa'.

T50 light tank. At more than double the weight of the T40 this light tank could not swim. It was armed with a 45 mm main gun, plus two machine guns and was designed both to support the infantry and to serve as a light battle tank for the cavalry. Unfortunately, it proved unsuitable for both these opposing roles and did not go into large scale production.

T60 light tank. When it was found that both the T40 and T50 were unsatisfactory, it was decided to develop a new light tank, based on the T40 chassis but not to make it amphibious. It had improved protection and entered full-scale production in 1941. Designed with the need to operate in snow specifically in mind, some 6,000 were produced before it was replaced by the T70.

T60A light tank (*Bottom right*). Young Soviet tank crewmen receiving their brand new light tanks, as Joseph Stalin's portrait looks on. The T60A was the improved production model with thicker frontal armour.

T30 light tank (*Far left*). Early in 1940, the Russians developed an amphibious light tank to replace the earlier designs, but it did not go into production. The prototype was called the T30 and it mounted a 20 mm cannon with a co-axial machine gun.

T40 light tank (*Near left*). The two-man crew of this little 6-ton amphibious tank pose proudly in immaculate black uniforms with highly polished leather accoutrements. The T40 looked very like the T30 and mounted either a 12.7 mm D ShK or 20 mm ShVaK gun, plus a co-axial machine gun. It had buoyancy tanks built into the hull and was driven in the water by a single, four-bladed propeller.

T70 light tank. More powerful, with thicker armour, the next member of the light tank family used the same basic chassis as the T60, but had thicker frontal armour, a more powerful gun (45 mm) and two power units arranged in tandem. Weighing just over 9 tons, it had a top speed of 32 mph. Over 8,000 were produced and the T70 chassis was also used to mount a 76.2 mm gun (see page 129). The photograph was taken in the Orel-Kursk area, where Hitler's summer offensive of 1943 was smashed.

SU37 anti-aircraft gun. The T70 chassis was also used as an anti-aircraft gun mount. There were two versions, one with a single 37 mm AA gun as seen here, the other with twin 37 mm AA guns.

Russian Medium Tanks

Now it was the Red Army's turn to attack. Well armed Russian infantry ride on the backs of a platoon of T34 medium tanks as they move in to attack a German position on the South Western front.

T34/76A medium tank. One of the most unpleasant surprises experienced by the Germans in Russia came some five months after the launching of Operation 'Barbarossa' in the shape of a new tank which inflicted heavy losses upon the Pzkpfw IIIs and IVs. General Guderian was so impressed with the new Russian tank that he thought the quickest way for the Germans to deal with the situation would be to copy it! It was, of course, the T34, one of the most important single elements in eventual Russian victory. Using a Christie-type suspension and mounting a 76.2 mm gun, the 28-ton tank had a crew of our and a top speed over 30 mph. Well armoured, robust and devoid of any frills, it was easily mass produced. The photograph shows a crew cleaning their main armament on the first production model, the T34/76A.

T34/76B medium tank. The next production model had a better gun, thicker armour so as to provide immunity against German 50 mm anti-tank guns and, in 1942, a cast turret. This photograph shows the earlier welded turret version.

T34. This head-on view of the T34 emphasises the almost pyramidical shape of the tank.

T34/76C medium tank. The third production version, the C model, had a larger turret with two hatches instead of the single, large, clumsy hatch of previous models.

T34/76D medium tank (*Above*). This much improved model had a new turret which was hexagonal in shape, with no overhang as on previous models. This did away with the 'bullet trap' which the overhang had created and also made it more difficult for enemy soldiers who had climbed onto the back to wedge Teller mines under the rear of the turret overhang.

T34 turret interior (*Right*). A good interior shot, showing the gunner's seat, telescope and gun controls.

T34/85 medium tank (*Below*). Towards the end of 1943 the T34 was made even more lethal by fitting the new 85 mm gun in an enlarged turret. The new gun had an effective range of 1,000 m and could penetrate the frontal armour of both Tiger and Panther at that range – or so the Russians claimed. The photograph shows the 1944 model which had a lighter turret.

T44 medium tank. In 1944 a new tank was designed, based upon the T34/85, but with a lower silhouette, more powerful armament – it was intended to mount the 100 mm gun – and thicker armour. Unfortunately, its designers did not have time to perfect the T44 and it suffered from mechanical problems. Nevertheless, the 35-ton tank did enter service and was used in limited numbers by the Red Army in 1945. It was replaced after the war by the T54.

T34 ARV. This turretless version of the T34 was used as an armoured recovery vehicle.

SU100 self-propelled gun (*Below*). The first gun to be mounted on the T34 chassis was the SU85 but, with the up-gunning of the T34 with the 85 mm, this SP became unnecessary and by September 1944 replacement had begun with the more powerful SU100, which mounted a new gun adapted from a pre-war naval gun. It had a greatly improved performance and could fire a 35 lb shell to a range of 21,000 yds. In the anti-tank role, it suffered from having very limited depression.

SU122 self-propelled gun (*Left*). Even more powerful than the SU100, the SU122 mounted a Model 1938 122 mm field howitzer on the T34 chassis to provide artillery fire support for armoured divisions. However, it was not effective against armoured vehicles and was withdrawn in late 1943.

Russian Heavy Tanks

KV1A heavy tank. The heavy tank with which Russia started World War 2 was a redesign of the T100, with one of the turrets eliminated. It was known as the KV1, named after the Russian Marshal Klimenti Voroshilov. It weighed some $43\frac{1}{2}$ tons and first saw active service in the Russo-Finnish war. It was replaced later in 1940 by the KV1A, which mounted a better gun with a higher muzzle velocity and firing a larger round – the 76.2 mm L/41.5 Model 40. This model was initially introduced just for tank platoon commanders but later most tanks were fitted with the more powerful gun.

KV1B heavy tank. Next in the line was the 1B, which was the 1A with an additional sheet of 20 mm armour bolted onto the upper part of the front hull, thus providing extra protection to the two crewmen located there (driver and hull gunner). The later production model of the 1B had a cast turret. The photograph shows the Leningrad tank factory working by night to speed up production.

KV1C heavy tank. This was the 1942 production model, with a cast turret, broader tracks with steel rimmed road wheels (due to a rubber shortage) and a machine gun mounting in the rear of the turret.

KV2A close-support tank. The close support version of the KV appeared in early 1941 and mounted a 152 mm howitzer in a large, slab sided turret, making it look very unwieldly (which it was) and a good 1½ feet taller than the contemporary KV1B and 1C. Its weight was over 53 tons and it had a crew of six.

KV85 heavy tank. After the 1C, the Russians produced the 1S, which was 5¼ tons lighter and 5 mph faster. This was followed by the KV85 which was armed with the 85 mm gun mounted in a larger cast turret and using the same chassis as the 1S. As the photograph shows, the commander's cupola was large and mushroom shaped. It came into service in 1943.

JS1 heavy tank. Russia began to develop a new tank in 1941. At that time, the requirement was for a four-man tank with an 85 mm gun and sufficient armour to keep out the German 50 mm anti-tank gun round, but with no significant increase in weight over the KV1 series. By the time it appeared in 1943 the main armament had been changed initially to 100 mm and then to 122 mm. As the photograph shows, the tank had a very good ballistic shape and a low silhouette and was extremely reliable.

JS2 heavy tank. The next model appeared in 1944, an improved model of the JS1, but there was little external difference. The gun was now 122 mm, making it the most powerfully armed tank in the world. It had a smaller cupola and some differences in the armour silhouette around the front hull.

JS3 heavy tank (*Left*). Coming into service in early 1945, the JS3, seen here on a Victory Parade in Berlin on 7 September 1945, had a much more streamlined shape, with a lower silhouette and a larger, tapered turret. It weighed under 50 tons, had a crew of four and a top speed of 23 mph. It went on in service long after the end of World War 2 in many Eastern Bloc armies and other armies all over the world.

SU152 self-propelled gun (*Below left*). Based upon the KV chassis, the SU152 mounted a 152 mm howitzer and first saw action in the Kursk area during early 1943. The Russian soldiers had a high regard for this SP, which did well against German heavy tanks and earned the name 'Conquering Beast'.

Victory! (*Below*). A Russian JS2 heavy tank gives a patrol a ride in the middle of Berlin after the German surrender. The Brandenberg Gate can be seen in the background.

World War Two
7 United States

Winston Churchill described the growth of the American Army in World War 2 as a 'prodigy of organisation'. Nowhere was this more apparent than in the field of armoured warfare. At the time of Pearl Harbor, the USA had only a handful of tanks in service and most of these were obsolete models. They also had little proven potential in tank design and production, while relatively few American officers were trained in the art of tank warfare. By 1945, however, they had built a staggering total of 88,410 tanks and proved themselves adept in their handling of armour. In 1943, for example, when wartime production was at its peak, an incredible 29,497 tanks were completed in one year alone! American tanks and other armoured fighting vehicles were used to equip a vast number of Allied armoured formations, while in their own Army and Marine Corps tanks were used in all theatres of war and American tank commanders earned themselves an enviable reputation for élan.

This vast scale of production was only made possible by the innate American ability for mass production on a scale which defied the imagination. They were, for example, designing and building factories to produce the tanks at the same time as they were designing the tanks themselves. Unfortunately, this mad rush for increased production led to basic errors – for example the production of light tanks was allowed to continue for far too long. Although the Honey/Stuart line was a decided improvement upon the tanks they replaced, their standard 37 mm gun was no better than the British 2-pdr and suffered from the same drawbacks. It was in the medium tank range where the Americans initially produced battle winning weapons, but were unable or unwilling to revise their ideas fast enough to keep pace with enemy armoured development. This was very apparent in that most important single characteristic of a tank, namely, *firepower*. When first produced, the 75 mm gun of the M3 and M4 did much to restore the tank *versus* tank balance and to give the Allies a weapon with a dual capability, which was more than a match for its German equivalent. It was hailed at the time as a war winner, especially when mounted in the ubiquitous Sherman. Reliable and robust, the new tank led the successful Allied advance across North Africa, but its vulnerability (not for nothing did its crews describe it as the 'Ronson Lighter' – it always lit first time) and lack of gunpower against the formidable German heavy tanks, Tiger and Panther, was glossed over. Later efforts were made to upgun to 76 mm but even the new weapon could still not penetrate the frontal armour of Panther, at over 500 yards. All too little effort was put into the production of heavy tanks, until far too late in the war. So the Pershing, with its excellent armour profile and formidable 90 mm gun, did not come into service until March 1945, three years after its German equivalent, Tiger 1.

As well as gun tanks, the Americans produced a bewildering array of specialised armoured vehicles, using the basic tank chassis as a starting point. The British did likewise, and I have deliberately tried to demonstrate this amazing range of 'funnies'.

One effect of the success of the German *Blitzkrieg* upon the US Army, was to make them look for more effective ways of stopping tanks. This led to the setting up of the separate Tank Destroyer Command, equipped with light, fast, hard hitting tank destroyers, always ready to seek out and destroy the enemy armour. Undoubtedly this new force lived up to its proud motto 'Seek, Strike, Destroy' and the TD proved itself highly effective when used correctly. However, overall battlefield experience showed that the light armoured tank destroyer with its open-topped turret was not as effective or as versatile as the tank. Consequently, the end of the war also saw the demise of the TD force.

'Armor as the ground arm of mobility, emerged from World War 2 with a lion's share of the credit for the Allied victory. Indeed armor enthusiasts at that time regarded the tank as the main weapon of the land army'. That quote from the official US history of World War 2, encapsulates the immediate post-war American thought on the AFV. How very different it was from their feelings at the start of the conflict.

M3 medium tank. The first American-built tanks to see action in World War 2 were the M3 light tanks and M3 medium tanks, which were shipped over to North Africa to equip the British Eighth Army. The first M3 Grants arrived in the Western Desert in 1942 at a time when the British were manning the Gazala Line, facing Rommel's Afrika Korps and his Italian Allies. The new tank, although essentially only a stop gap, before the arrival of the ubiquitous Sherman, at long last provided British armour with a gun that could deal with enemy tanks and anti-tank guns much more effectively than their 2-pdrs. Here a Grant passes a shell torn building in Italy in April 1945. The Grant was distinguishable from the American version of the M3 medium tank, the Lee, as it did not have the tall commander's cupola.

American Light Tanks

M2A4 light tank. US Marines and supporting tanks pause on the beach of Guadalcanal Island in the Solomons soon after landing there in the summer of 1942. The light tank is the 11½-ton M2A4 which came into service in 1939. It was armed with a 37 mm gun and five machine guns, one co-axial, two in side sponsons, another in the hull and finally one on an AA mounting on the rear of the turret – what a lot of firepower for such a small AFV! The M2A4 was the first tank to be mass produced in the USA in World War 2.

M3 light tank. The M2A4 was effectively a prototype for the next light tank, the M3, which had many of its features, such as the single rotating turret and 37 mm gun. The M3 was designed in the spring of 1940. The main requirement was for thicker armour, putting the weight up to 12.3 tons and requiring stronger suspension. Nicknamed the Honey, the M3 first saw action with the British Army in the Western Desert where this photograph was taken. Here the 8th King's Royal Irish Hussars try out their new tanks. The tank was also officially known as the Stuart 1 in the British Army.

M3A1 with Satan flame gun. In late January 1944, some twenty Ronson Canadian vehicle flamethrowers were taken to the Central Pacific area. Replacing the main armament of M3 light tanks, they were used to great effect to winkle Japanese out of pillboxes and other strong points.

M3 with welded turret. The first production models were of a rivetted construction, but they were soon followed by a welded turret, still seven sided in shape like its predecessor. All five machine guns are clearly visible on this Honey.

Stuart 1 in Canadian Service (*Below left*). Taken on training, 'somewhere in England', is an M3 on which the sponson machine guns have been removed – this was a good idea as they could not be properly aimed and must have wasted a great deal of ammunition.

M3s in foreign service (*Below right*). These M3s with welded turrets and rivetted hulls belong to the Brazilian Army.

M3A1 with wading gear (*Above*). The Stuart III, as the British called the M3A1, is seen here fitted with wading gear designed to enable it to wade ashore from a landing craft.

M3E3 light tank (*Top left*). An experimental model, which had twin Cadillac engines, a turret basket and other modifications. It was the prototype for the M5.

M3A1 light tank (*Bottom left*). The next model put into production in the summer of 1941 was the M3A1. It had no side sponson machine guns, and no commander's cupola. It had a turret basket and power traverse.

M3A3 light tank (*Below*). Final model of the M3 series was the M3A3 (Stuart V in British parlance). It had a larger turret and, having done away with the side sponsons, room for extra fuel tanks and ammunition stowage.

M5 light tank (*Top left*). The end of the Honey line was the M5 – they missed out the 'M4' designation so as not to cause confusion with the M4 Sherman. It first came off the assembly line in March 1942. The British called it the Stuart VI. It weighed about 15 tons and was powered by two Cadillac engines, giving a top speed of 40 mph.

M5 light tank (*Bottom*). The American Army and the US Marine Corps made full use of tanks even in the jungles of the Pacific theatre. Here a pair of M5 light tanks move forward on the Arawe Peninsula of New Britain Island, March 1944 ready to help the accompanying infantry to mop up. Note the heavily constructed log pillbox which had just fallen into their hands.

Satan flame gun in action (*Above*). Good photograph of a US Marine M3A1 flame-thrower getting to work on a Japanese position on Saipan.

M3 with AA turret (*Left*). An M3 was fitted with a Maxson turret containing four .50 cal Brownings. Tested in 1942, it was eventually rejected in preference for the same mounting on a half-track.

M5 with Culin hedgerow cutter (*Above left*). This device was designed to cut through the thick bocage hedgerows of Normandy, many of the metal prongs being made locally from the German beach defences.

M8 Howitzer Motor Carriage (*Above right*). The M8 mounted a 75 mm howitzer and was ideal for the job of close-support. It was widely used, until replaced by the M7 HMC (Sherman with 105 mm howitzer).

T8E1 reconnaissance vehicle (*Centre left*). A number of M5s were converted in 1944 into light recce vehicles, by removing the turret and fitting a ring mounted .50 cal machine gun in its place.

Stuart recce vehicle (*Bottom left*). This was the British conversion of the Stuart V, minus its turret, with various pintle-mounted armament. A similar conversion was the Kangaroo, which had seats fitted inside the turretless hull for infantry. The photograph was taken in Arezzo, Italy in July 1944.

A dummy Honey (*Below*). Dummy vehicles of all types were used extensively by both sides in the Western Desert to fool enemy recce 'planes.

M22 light tank. Designed as an airborne tank, the little M22 Locust only saw operational service with the British Army, with whom it was used in small numbers by 6th Airborne Reconnaissance Regiment during the Rhine Crossing. Here, a Locust leaves a Hamilcar glider, which had been specially designed to carry the British light airborne tank, the Tetrarch. Locust was armed with a 37 mm gun and a co-axial machine gun.

M24 light tank. Undoubtedly the best light tank of the war was the M24 Chaffee, named after General Adna Chaffee, the 'Father of the US Armored Force'. It was a five-man tank, but was normally manned by only four men due to manpower shortages. The main armament was a powerful 75 mm gun which had been adapted from the heavy aircraft cannon as used in the B-25G Mitchell bomber. It remained the standard US light tank long after the end of the war.

Device M20 fitted to an M24. The M20 swimming device comprised fore and aft pontoons to give floatation, plus grousers on the tracks to give better propulsion in the water, and had rudders on the rear.

T77E1 Gun Motor Carriage. Work on this anti-aircraft gun mount was begun in 1943, but the project did not go into production and was abandoned at the end of the war.

American Medium Tanks

M3 medium tank General Lee (*Top left*). M3s belonging to the US Army on training in England. The British called the standard M3 the Lee, after General Robert E. Lee. Its main armament was the sponson mounted 75 mm gun which only had limited traverse. In the fully rotating turret on the top of the tank was a 37 mm and co-axial machine gun. There were up to three more machine guns – one in the commander's cupola (not fitted here) and either one or two fixed machine guns firing through the front plate (the earlier production models had two). The Lee had a crew of seven, a top speed of 24 mph, weighed about 28 tons and had armour some $2\frac{1}{2}$ ins thick.

M3 medium tank General Grant (*Above right*). The British version of the M3 was purchased under Lend-Lease by a special Tank Commission. It differed from the Lee in having a larger turret with a bulge at the rear to take a radio set. This meant that the operator could also act as loader for the 37 mm, and one crew member less was needed to man the Grant as the British version was called (after General Ulysses S. Grant). The commander's cupola was also dispensed with, thus reducing the overall height by some 4 ins. A column of Grants is seen here under training in the Western Desert.

An M3 negotiates a steep slope. Note the 75 mm gun barrel has been fitted with a counterweight to balance the short barrelled M2 gun.

Full frontal (*Top left*). A tank transporter crew pull out their winch rope before attaching it to a Grant in a typical Western Desert setting. The photograph gives an excellent front view of the Grant, note the high angle of elevation possible on the 37 mm gun (+60°). The 75 mm could only traverse through an arc of 60°, and a great deal of the tank's 10 ft 3 ins height had to be exposed in order to bring the gun into action.

Have they gone yet? (*Left*). A camouflaged Grant in the Western Desert 'pretends' that it is a lorry. The hessian-made exterior was mounted on a removable framework and proved to be most effective.

M31 armoured recovery vehicle. A tank recovery vehicle (ARV in British parlance) starts to lift a ditched Sherman. The M31 or T2 as it was called, had its guns removed – the barrel sticking out of the sponson is a dummy – and was fitted with a rear mounted boom and a winch with a 60,000 lb pull.

Grants in the Far East (*Left*). The M3 was also used in the Far East, the 3rd Carabiniers being equipped with both Lees and Grants in Burma, where they did excellent work, bunker bashing and supporting the infantry. There was little enemy tank opposition encountered in the campaign.

Grant ARV II (*Top right*). A British Grant ARV carries a scout car on its boom with ease.

Grant CDL (*Centre right*). When the M3 was replaced by the Sherman M4, a number of British Grants were fitted with a similar Canal Defence Light to that which had been fitted earlier on to the Matilda CDL. As the photograph shows, the turret was removed and replaced with an armoured searchlight housing, sporting a dummy wooden gun, but also containing a machine gun. The sponson-mounted 75 mm was still retained. As the Bullshead symbol on the front of this CDL shows, the AFV was part of the famous British 79th Armoured Division. The Americans called the CDL the Shop Tractor to disguise its true role. One of the most secret inventions of World War 2, it was never used to anything like its true potential.

T36 Gun Motor Carriage (*Bottom right*). This anti-aircraft tank mounted a 40 mm gun in a power-operated turret (the gun is seen here at maximum elevation). After nearly two years work the project was cancelled in July 1943 for various reasons, in particular because of the inadequate amunition stowage space (only room for 100 rounds).

M3 Lee with flame gun (*Below*). This M3 has had its guns removed and the 37 mm replaced by a long barrelled flame gun, the E3. The arrangement did not get further than the trial stage.

Grant Scorpion III flail. The British Army also converted the Grant into a mine-clearing tank, using the Scorpion flail, as fitted to the Matilda and Valentine. It saw service in the Middle East, and also in Sicily and Italy.

In deep down-under (*Bottom left*). An interesting shot of a Grant in Australia fitted up with deep wading gear.

Cargo Carrier M30 (*Above*). Remove the 155 mm gun and recoil spade from the M3-based M12 motor gun carriage and replace with cargo space and a ring-mounted .50 cal machine gun and the result is the M30 cargo carrier, used as the limber for the M12, carrying ammunition, stores and part of the gun grew.

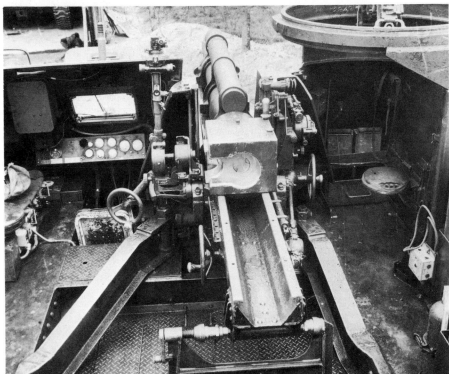

M7 Howitzer Motor Carriage (*Above*). One of the most successful conversions of the M3 chassis (and later the M4) was the mounting on it of a 105 mm howitzer. The open topped superstructure had a ring mounted .50 cal machine gun on top of the commander's cupola on the righthand side of the vehicle. The gun crew was seven (including vehicle commander and driver) and some 69 rounds of 105 mm ammunition could be carried on board. Here, a French manned M7 takes on extra ammunition, during a shoot against the enemy positions in the Rhine Valley in December 1944. Note the stack of empty cases at the side of the HMC. The British named the M7 the 105 mm SP Priest.

M7 105 mm howitzer (*Left*). An internal view of an M7, showing the breech end of the 105 mm howitzer, the vehicle commander's cupola to its right and the driver's seat to the left.

M12 Gun Motor Carriage. The Americans also mounted a 155 mm gun onto the M3 chassis. It was designed in 1941, first produced in 1942, but did not see combat until 1944, being used for training in the meantime. Here, M12s, using ramps to obtain maximum elevation, shell the village of Bildohen, south west of Aachen, which was part of the Siegfried Line.

The Sherman M4 medium tank (*Left*). Following on from the M3 came the medium tank T6, which incorporated much of the basic M3 but with the main gun in a centrally placed all round traversing turret. In October 1941 the T6 was standardised as the medium tank M4. Over the years many different types of Sherman were produced, as the photographs which follow show. The tank weighed some 30 tons, although later Marks went up to nearly 35 tons. The main armament was a 75 mm gun, later replaced by a 76 mm, plus three machine guns (one ball mounted in the front hull, one co-axial and one .50 on an AA mount). More Shermans were produced than any other tank in World War 2, and it fought in just about every theatre and was used by nearly all the Allied armies. It would be true to say that the Sherman tank was the tank that won the war.

Sherman M4 medium tank (*Right*). The most widely used Allied tank of World War 2 was undoubtedly the Sherman. A staggering total of 49,234 Sherman gun tanks was built. Many were used by the British, like this OP tank churning up the dust as it passes a column of infantrymen in the Italian Appenines in September 1944.

Sherman M4A1. The British Tank Mission were quick to order the new tank and the very first one to be shipped to the UK was this M4A1, which came off the assembly line established for the British contract at the Lima Locomotive Works in February 1942. It was the second tank ever to be built at Lima. It was armed with a short barrelled 75 mm M2 gun fitted with two counterweights, as the new M3 gun was not available. This photograph was taken shortly after its arrival in UK when it was on display on Horseguards Parade in London. The name *Michael* on its side is in honour of Michael Dewar, head of the British Tank Mission. Note the three machine guns in the front plate; the fixed pair were later removed.

Sherman M4A2. In late 1941, work started on a modified version of the M4, which was to be powered by twin General Motors diesel engines instead of the Continental R975 petrol engine as in the M4 and M4A1. The photograph shows one of the first production models.

M4 infantry support. Advancing through the snow during the winter of 1944, a Sherman, hastily camouflaged with whitewash, supports GIs of the US 7th Army in the Colmar area of France.

Up-gunning the Sherman. Clearly the most important requirement for the Sherman after it had been in service for some time, was to up-gun it so that it would be able to knock out the heavier German tanks. The Ordnance Department developed the 76 mm gun which had a muzzle velocity, when using the APCM62 projectile, of 2,600 ft per sec as compared with 2,030 ft per sec of the 75 mm M3 and M6 guns. Tested in August 1942, the gun was standardised and Shermans re-equipped with the new weapon had 76M1 put after their nomenclature. Although more powerful than the 75 mm, the new gun was unfortunately still unable to penetrate the frontal armour of either Panther or Tiger.

Sherman Firefly. One gun that *could* do this, however, was the British 17-pdr. The conversion produced the most effective Sherman of the war, the Sherman Firefly. Top priority was put onto the up-gunning programme in 1944 but, by the time D-Day arrived there were only sufficient Fireflies to issue on the basis of one per tank troop.

Sherman with 105 mm howitzer. For close-support work it was decided to mount a 105 mm howitzer and two M4A4s were modified in November 1942. As the photograph shows, the howitzer had to have a very large mantlet to cover the bulky experimental howitzer.

M4 (105 mm). The eventual L/25 105 mm howitzer was less bulky and a normal mantlet was fitted as seen here on this M4 (105 mm). Ammunition for the howitzer included 42 lb HE shells and all other standard 105 mm howitzer rounds, the HEAT projectile being able to penetrate about 4 ins of armour. Some 68 rounds were carried.

T31 demolition tank. This strange looking experimental vehicle mounted a 7.2 in rocket projector on either side of a 105 mm howitzer. It only reached prototype stage. The photograph also shows the improved type of suspension which was fitted to late production M4A3s, namely Horizontal Volute Spring Suspension (HVSS) which was introduced from mid-1944 and replaced the normal Vertical Volute type.

T14 assault tank. Increased protection was just as important as firepower, and it was with with some justification that the Sherman crews wryly called their tank 'The Ronson Lighter' – because it lit first time! This was especially important for assault operations and the result was the T14 assault tank, nicknamed 'Jumbo' (although this one also appears to be called 'Baby'!) – it weighed in at 47 tons, about 12 tons heavier than the average Sherman. The T14 did not reach production although one was sent to the UK and can still be seen at the Bovington Tank Museum, Dorset.

Trackplate protection. One partly effective way of obtaining protection was to festoon the tank with spare trackplates as seen here in a column of Canadian-manned Shermans, pushing through Holland towards the V-2 sites.

Grousers. In order to improve cross country mobility in soft terrain, wider tracks were needed. First $32\frac{1}{2}$ in grousers were added to the tracks and then 37 in ones were installed on this M4A3. Finally a set of 39 in grousers were tried out. Despite the extra weight the ground pressure was reduced.

Plastic armour installation. The deadly effect of the German lightweight man-portable hollow charge weapons, such as the Panzerfaust, resulted in trials of applique armour such as this plastic armour which was fitted to an M4A3 (HVSS), increasing its weight by some 8 tons. Testing continued after the war.

'Just like the real thing'. There were even dummy Shermans!

Water-crossing gear. The ability to get across water obstacles without the aid of a bridge was a valuable asset. Here, a partly waterproofed Sherman gingerly fords a river in Italy. The fording depth of the Sherman, without preparation, was 40 ins.

Waterproofing for an assault landing. Deeper water required full waterproofing, sealing up all possible holes and fitting waterproof covers over vulnerable parts. Note the tall engine breather stack, a good deal larger than the one used in the river crossing photograph.

159

A clean pair of tracks. Dry landing for this fully waterproofed Sherman, arriving in France not long after D-Day. *Hurricane* was able to get ashore without getting even a little damp.

T6 flotation device. The method of flotation most favoured by the US Army was the use of floats, such as this type which was tested early in 1944 and then used in the Pacific theatre. It comprised a series of compartmented steel floats attached to the front, rear and both sides of the tank. The compartments were filled with plastic foam covered with waterproof cellophane. The tracks provided propulsion at about 4 mph in the water. Twin rudders (not fitted here) were used to steer via control ropes to the turret hatch.

Sherman DD medium tank. One of the most closely guarded secrets of the war was the invention by Nicholas Straussler of the Duplex Drive tank. This comprised a collapsible screen which was raised around the waterproofed tank, using rubber tubes carrying compressed air. Struts then held it in place. Propellers, seen at the rear of this DD as it enters the water were driven by a power take-off from the main engine and provided the necessary propulsion.

US Marines land on Iwo Jima (*Right*). A graphic picture of the landing area shows the full use made by the Americans of armour in the Pacific, with M4s.

Sherman DD with screen collapsed (*Left*). A complete brigade of Sherman DDs was used on D-Day in the British and Canadian sectors. They were the only gun tanks to get ashore so their support was invaluable. In the US sector, most of the DDs foundered in the rough seas. The existence of DD tanks was not made public until September 1945. This photograph shows a Sherman DD with the screen folded and the propellers in the raised position.

Preparing for D-Day (*Right*). Sherman DDs take part in large-scale landing exercises on the South coast. Note that, once the screen has been collapsed, the tank can use its main armament even when it is still in the water. The 79th Armoured Division sign is clearly visible on the turret of the nearest Sherman DD.

Sherman BARV. An extremely useful vehicle during beach landings was the Beach Armoured Recovery Vehicle, seen here passing a column of Shermans waiting to load onto LCTs prior to D-Day. Tested in December 1943, this adaptation of the British Sherman ARV (see later) was very successful.

Tank Recovery Vehicle M32B3 (*Right*). An excellent photograph of a recovery vehicle showing its boom fully extended and raised. This version was based on the Sherman M4A3 chassis, with HVSS.

Sherman BARV in action. Watched by a motley collection of spectators, a Sherman BARV tows a lorry ashore on to the Normandy beaches. This was the primary use of the BARV.

Sherman Dozer (*Right*). When official dozers were not available a number of ad hoc dozers did yeoman service, like this one on the Italian front. The blade and hydraulic gear from a D8 Dozer having been 'borrowed' to fit onto an M4.

Tank Recovery Vehicle M32. A prime requirement for any armoured unit is for repair and recovery, so it is essential that unit fitters have a vehicle sufficiently powerful to deal with the tanks that they support, be they broken down, ditched or damaged by enemy action. The Sherman tank recovery vehicle was basically a tank from which the turret and gun had been removed and replaced by a fixed turret which mounted a powerful 60,000 lb winch, jib and an 81 mm mortar to fire smoke to cover recovery operations (not fitted in this photograph of an M32B1).

Sherman ARV I. The British also developed recovery vehicles based on the Sherman by removing the turret and rearranging the hull stowage. Here, a Sherman ARV I waits near the approaches to the Rhine in case it is needed during the crossing operations on 24 March 1945.

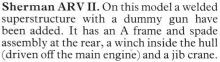

Sherman ARV II. On this model a welded superstructure with a dummy gun have been added. It has an A frame and spade assembly at the rear, a winch inside the hull (driven off the main engine) and a jib crane.

M1 Dozer Blade. A special dozer blade was designed for the Sherman and is seen here in Western Normandy. The blade was 124 ins wide (138 in on later models) and weighed 3½ tons.

M1 Dozer Blade. This turretless Sherman M4A1 has also been fitted with an M1 blade. Note the armoured cover over the lifting gear.

Sherman OP/Command tank (*Left*). This Sherman OP tank was photographed in Italy in July 1944. In order to make room for the extra radios needed, the gun was removed and replaced by a wooden dummy barrel. The extra radio aerials, cable reels and impedimenta can be seen on the outside of the AFV.

E1 Anti-Personnel Tank Projector (*Right*). This was not strictly a flame thrower per se as it consisted of four small projectors which could be fired en mass or singly and were fitted to the sides of the tank. They were designed to deal with *Kamikaze* type of attacks at short range by suicide troops. It was also called the Scorpion.

T52 Multiple Gun Motor Carriage (*Left*). Designed in 1942 by the Firestone Tire and Rubber Co., this multiple anti-aircraft gun mount comprised a 40 mm AA gun flanked by a pair of .50 cal machine guns. It had a crew of four, two in the ball-type turret. Tests showed tracking rates against low flying aircraft were too slow, so the project was cancelled in late 1944.

M3–4–3 flame thrower (*Below*). This type of flame thrower was bow-mounted in place of the .30 cal machine gun in the ball mount. It had a range of about 60 yds. Here, a demonstration is given to some infantry officers in Luxembourg in November 1944.

POA–CWS–H5 flame thrower (*Below*). The flame thrower was mounted co-axially with the main armament, and the fuel container was inside the turret.

Cowcatcher rocket launcher. This was an early type of rocket launcher with the battery of rockets mounted on the front of the tank *a la* cowcatcher on a train.

T34 Calliope rocket launcher. The T34 had sixty tubes, each 90 ins long and firing 4.5 in rockets. On the tank in this photograph the elevation arm has been removed from the gunbarrel and attached to the gunshield. This enabled the main armament to be fired with the launcher still in place.

M17 rocket launcher (*Top left*). Also called the T40, this 7.2 in multiple rocket launcher, carried twenty rockets in two equal rows. Nicknamed the Whizzbang, it was used in action during the invasion of Southern France and in the Italian campaign.

Pram Scorpion mine exploder (*Top right*). A later development of the Scorpion IV, the Pram Scorpion used the tank engine to power the flail rotor via large attachments on the sprockets. It did not enter service.

T99 rocket launcher (*Left*). Yet another type of mounting was the T99 which had four banks of rocket tubes, two on either side of the turret. It fired fin-stabilised 4.5 in rockets, 44 in all.

Sherman 60 lb rocket projectile installation (*Below left*). A British rocket system involved fitting on either side of the turret a launcher rail to take a 60 lb aircraft rocket projectile as used by Hawker Typhoon aircraft, and based on a 6 in Naval shell. Men of the Guards Armoured Division are seen here just near Bremen in their rocket-mounted Shermans.

Sherman Marquis (*Above*). Another variation of the Scorpion, the Marquis was produced by removing the turret and replacing it with an armoured housing to protect the auxiliary engines. It did not enter service.

Sherman Scorpion IV mine exploder (*Bottom left*). This flail equipment was very similar to that mounted on the Grant Scorpion IV. It had two auxiliary engines to drive the chain flail which meant that the ARV was very wide and difficult to get across bridges.

Sherman Crab Mark I. Coming ashore on the invasion beaches from an LCT is the most successful mine-clearing device of all, the Crab. Three Regiments of 79th Armoured Division, under the direct command of 30th Armoured Brigade, were equipped with Sherman Crabs. They were used to great effect not just on the Normandy beaches but also throughout the North West European campaign.

Sherman Crab Mark II. Good picture of a Sherman Crab in the process of flailing a gap through a minefield. The Mk II had various improvements, but did not get into service in time for many to be used by 79th Armoured Division.

Sherman Crab Mark II. This photograph of the Crab Mk II shows the direction keeping lights and lane marking equipment on the rear of the Sherman V (M4A4). The main improvement was to the flail arms so that the drum remained at a constant height above the ground and thus the beating chains would deal with any mines buried in depressions which would have been missed by the Mk I.

Sherman with AMRCR. The anti-mine reconnaissance castor roller was just like the one fitted to the Churchill tank. Rollers were carried in a frame in front of the tank and exploded the mines by pressure. It never reached operational service.

Sherman CIRD. Another type of roller device was the Canadian Indestructible Roller Device. Two patterns were fitted to the Sherman, one with $15\frac{1}{2}$ in rollers, the other with 18 in rollers. The CIRD was also fitted to Churchill. The one in the photograph is also fitted with 'Flying Bangalore Torpedos' used for blowing gaps in barbed wire, etc.

Sherman with Lulu. Seen here in its operating position, Lulu was an electrical mine detecting device. There were mine detector coils in each of the wooden drums which registered on an indicator inside the tank when they passed over a mine.

Pancake mine clearing device. This odd looking machine used standard conveyor components to carry explosive charges along its 22 ft arms. The charges were then lowered almost to ground level and set off remotely, blasting any mines below them. Some 160 charges could be carried in the tank and this was estimated to be sufficient to clear a gap 800 ft long. It was demonstrated in February 1945 and then discontinued in favour of the demolition hose and the multiple rocket launcher.

Aunt Jemima. The production pilot model of the Mine Exploder T1E3, which was put into production and some 75 built. It was one of the most successful roller devices produced and saw service in North West Europe and Italy. Sometimes a second tank had to be used to push 'Aunt Jemima' along.

Mine excavator T5. This was developed to scoop up the mines and deposit them to one side of the cleared lane. The photograph shows the T5E2 excavator in action. The last model in the series, the T5E3 was put into production in 1945 and 100 were produced. They saw service in the Pacific area.

Mine exploder T9. The heavy spudded 6 ft roller was pushed in front of the tank. The photograph shows exactly what happened in heavy going – the tank bogged down! Production was discontinued in September 1944.

Mine exploder T10. This bizarre looking device originally had tricycle roller units which were controlled remotely from a tank following behind. It was then developed into a self-contained unit, with a Sherman hull and turret above the rollers. It was tested in 1944 but proved to be unwieldy to use.

Spigot Mortar Attachment. After trying out 60 mm spigot mortars for destroying mines and obstacles in assault landings, it was decided to mount five spigots on the front of an M4A4 for experimental purposes only.

Mine exploder T12. The next step was to mount 25 60 mm spigot mortars on a turretless Sherman. When fired, a path 20 ft wide and 250 ft deep could be cleared, starting about 150 ft in front of the AFV.

Mine Resistant Vehicle T15. With extra belly and side armour, no turret, heavy duty tracks and suspension units reinforced with armoured brackets, the T15 was designed to drive across minefields – an indestructible tank! The photograph shows the second of the three models built, which were all very similar. Work started in September 1944, but development was abandoned at the end of the war.

Sherman fascine carrier. One of the oldest methods of getting across a small gap was to drop into it a fascine made of brushwood. This particular fascine carrier was a modification of the Sherman, by removing the turret to permit it to carry two or three fascines.

Sherman Twaby Ark. This bridging M4 was very similar to the Churchill Ark, with trackway extending over the top of the turretless hull. Hinged ramps were fitted at each end which were supported by posts. A second vehicle was needed to pull up the posts and ramps once the Twaby had taken up its position: note the wires attached to these posts. It was only used for training.

Sherman Octopus. This was an experimental type of bridge designed by the British and developed from the Sherman Twaby Ark.

M40 Gun Motor Carriage. Developed early in 1944, 'Big Shot' was a formidable 155 mm gun mounted on an M4A3 chassis. The tank chassis had to be widened slightly and the mounting was made so that it could accept either the 155 mm gun or the 8 in howitzer. With this latter armament it was known as the M4 GMC. The first time the M40 was used in action was during the bombardment of Koln.

Medium tank M7. It is difficult to decide whether this AFV should appear in the medium or light tank section. It started life as the light tank T7E2, a larger and more powerful light tank to replace the M3 series. It was to be armed with a 37 mm gun, but before it was completed it had been decided to up-gun to 57 mm, using an adaptation of the British 6-pdr gun as fitted to the Canadian-built Ram Mk II. So a Ram turret ring was incorporated and the tank was completed in June 1942. Later, the Armored Force asked if it could be modified to take a 75 mm gun. This was agreed even though the turret had to be redesigned. The other major change was to increase its armour thickness to 63 mm, thus putting the weight up to 25 tons and effectively taking it out of the light tank class. It was reclassified as the Medium Tank M7 and an order was placed for 3,000. However, in the meantime the pilot model had been fully tested and found now to be underpowered as its combat weight had crept up to 29 tons. While this was taking place, the Sherman had gone into full production and so it was decided to halt production of the M7 after only a handful had been built.

Medium tank T22. As soon as the M4 was in production, work started on its replacement. There followed a number of different series of tanks, starting with the T20 and leading on to the T22. Three differing models of the T20 were built, one with a 76 mm gun and HVSS, one with a 75 mm automatic gun and HVSS and the third with a 3 in gun and a torsion bar suspension. Chrysler were then asked to build two further pilot models, very like the T20 except that they were to have a five-speed mechanical transmission, just like the Sherman. One of these two was later converted to take the new 75 mm automatic gun and designated the T22E1. It is seen here with its enlarged turret, space being required for an automatic loader with separate magazines for AP and HE ammunition.

173

Medium tank T23. A parallel project to the T22 series was the T23, which had the same vertical volute spring suspension as Sherman, plus electric transmission. As with the T22, three types of gun – 76 mm, 75 mm automatic and 3 in – were specified. The photograph shows the T23-2, the second pilot model.

Medium tank T25. When the T20 series was at the design stage it had been suggested that a 90 mm gun should be specially designed for use in tanks. By early 1943, such a weapon was in existence and approval was given to fit a number of T23 trials vehicles with the new gun. Some would have the same armoured protection as the T23E3 and be designated T25, the rest would have increased armour and be called the T26. The T25 was over 40 tons, while T26 was about 5 tons heavier. Two pilot models of the T25 were built by Chrysler, one of which is seen here in January 1944. Note that it has HVSS and a much heavier turret than the T23.

Medium tank T25E1. The photograph shows a production model of the T25, which was designated T25E1. Some 40 were built, but only ever used for tests and development work. Armed with a 90 mm gun, it had a crew of five and a top speed of about 30 mph. In view of the coming invasion of Europe and the need for a more heavily armoured tank, the T25 was dropped in preference to the next series, T26.

Medium tank T26. Last of this string of medium tank developments was the T26. It was very like the T25, but heavier and better armoured. After various design changes to the transmission, ten vehicles were built for test purposes and scheduled as the T26E1. It was similar to the T25E1, but with broader tracks. It was also some 6 in wider and had thicker armour, 100 mm instead of 87 mm. Its weight had risen to such an extent as to exclude it from the medium tank range and in June 1944 it was reclassified as the Heavy Tank T26E. As such it was the prototype of the Pershing M26, which will be covered later.

American Heavy Tanks

Heavy tank M6. Until the start of World War 2 the USA had shown little interest in heavy tanks, one major reason being the difficulty of transporting such vehicles, especially overseas. However, the success of German armour and the obvious vulnerability and lack of firepower of the standard light and medium tanks, led to a recommendation to develop a heavy tank in the 50-ton class. Designed in 1940, the M6 heavy tank weighed about 56 tons and was armed with a 76.2 mm gun, with a 37 mm mounted co-axially, plus a total of four .50 cal and two .30 cal machine guns. Its armour was 5 in thick and it had a top speed of nearly 25 mph. At the time of construction – the pilot model was completed in December 1941 – it was the most powerful tank in the world. The Armored Force were not impressed with the new tank, and, after testing, concluded that it was too heavy, did not have a large enough main armament and suffered from transmission problems. Some 40 vehicles were built but they were only used for trial purposes.

Heavy tank M26. As mentioned in the medium tank section, the T26 series was the outcome of reclassifying the T25 as a heavy tank in June 1944. T26E3 was the designation given to the production model of the T26E1 which was later standardised as the M26 Pershing heavy tank. Weighing about 41 tons, with a 90 mm main gun, $4\frac{1}{2}$ in armour on the front turret and a top speed of 30 mph, the new tank was just about a match for the Tiger, produced some years earlier. It was the most powerful American tank to see combat in World War 2.

Tiger Killer. One of the very first Pershings to see action is pictured here with its triumphant crew after they had knocked out a Tiger 1 and two Pzkpfw IVs at Elsdorf, Germany in late February 1945. The 90 mm knocked out the two Panzer IVs at a range of 1,200 yds with just one round each. (Photograph supplied by Lt Col Elmer Gray.)

M26E1. Front view of this M26E1 gives a good impression of the powerful 90 mm gun. This particular model mounted the T54 gun, which used slightly longer ammunition, and had a new recoil system. It was designed to try to match the hitting power of the German 88 mm and two pilot models were built in 1945, but no production order followed. Wartime production of the M26 totalled 1,436.

T26E4. Another development was the T26E4, seen here. It was armed with a new 90 mm gun, the T15E2, which had a longer barrel and fired separate ammunition with a heavier charge. The longer barrel had to be balanced by a counterweight in the turret. Production of 1,000 T26E4 was approved, but only a handful were built before the end of the war.

Pershing with T121 mount (*Below*). Another way to add to Pershing's firepower was the installation of the T121 mount, containing two .50 (or .30) cal machine guns. The drawback was, of course, the increased height.

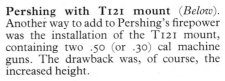

Super Pershing (*Left*). One ad hoc improvement to the firepower and protection of the Pershing was effected in the field by 3rd Armored Division. This 'Super Pershing', as seen here, had the new T15E1 gun with two large recoil cylinders containing coil springs fitted externally on top of the gun. An 80 mm plate from a German Panther tank has been welded onto the gun shield and more plate added to the front of the hull.

Pershing with rockets. One way of increasing the Pershing's hitting power was to install pods of rocket launchers. Four pods, each containing eleven 4.5 in rockets, were fitted to the turret. They could be fired singly or on automatic, a salvo taking just seven seconds.

177

Heavy tank T28. America did also try out a superheavy tank. This enormous 85-ton monster was the largest and heaviest American-designed tank of World War 2. It was also called the T95 GMC because its 105 mm gun had only limited traverse of 10° either side. Only two were built and the project was terminated in 1947.

Heavy tank T30. Following on from the M26 were various tanks, designed primarily to deal with the enemy heavy tanks, such as the Royal Tiger, and to attack the heavier fortified positions that were being met inside German territory. The T29, T30, T32 and T34 heavy tanks were produced. The T30, seen here, mounted a 155 mm gun and was powered by an 810 hp Continental engine. The T29 had a 105 mm gun and a 750 hp Ford engine.

Heavy tank T32 (*Left*). The T32 was an improved version of the M26 Pershing, with a lengthened hull, thicker armour (up to 200 mm on the front), an improved 90 mm gun and an up-rated engine. It weighed about 60 tons and was the last of the 1945 heavies produced. The T34 pilot models were not delivered until 1947 although they had been approved for development before the end of the war. In essence, the T34 was the T29–30 series, designed to take the 120 mm gun.

M10 tank destroyer (*Right*). An M10 tank destroyer – sometimes called the Wolverine – uses the corner of a ruined building to provide extra cover as it supports Free French Forces on their way to cross the Lauter River into the German village of Schriebenhardt, March 1945.

American Tank Destroyers

T35 Gun Motor Carriage (*Above*). The prototype for the M10 tank destroyer series was the T35 GMC, which mounted a 3 in gun in an open-topped, circular, welded turret on a Sherman M4A2 hull. Work on this model began in August 1942. It overtook various projects which had mounted 3 in guns on the M3 medium chassis.

M10 Gun Motor Carriage (*Left*). This was the first really successful tank destroyer in the US Army. The turret was five-sided (compare with the last photograph). It could carry 54 rounds of 3 in ammunition. It had a top speed of 30 mph and weighed about 30 tons. Note the counterweight which was added to the rear of the turret. A total of 5,000 M10s was built by Grand Blanc Arsenal between September 1942 and December 1943. A second version, the M10A1, used the M4A3 chassis a further 1,400 were built by Grand Blanc and Ford.

M10 Achilles. The British up-gunned some of the M10 and M10A1s which they received from America by fitting their highly lethal 17-pdr. The resulting TD was known as Achilles. Note the counterweight at the end of the barrel just behind the muzzle brake.

M35 Prime Mover. This conversion of the M10A1 had the turret removed and was used for towing 155 mm and 240 mm field guns. This evocative picture was taken in France in 1945.

M36 (*Above*). This view shows the large turret bustle on the rear to balance the M36's heavier gun. Like all the TDs, the M36 was often used as a tank, but it had thinner armour and an open top so one of the improvements subsequently made was a folding armoured top.

M36 Gun Motor Carriage. Most powerfully armed of all American tank destroyers was the M36 which mounted a 90 mm gun in place of the 3 in of the M10. Trials took place in 1943 with an M10 and it was proved to be quite successful. The only problem was the weight of the new gun which necessitated a new turret design. Standardised in July 1944, demand for it increased greatly after the battles in Normandy had shown that the 90 mm was the best US weapon to deal with enemy tanks. So, instead of just using M4A3 tank hulls, they had to use some M10s (TD then known as M36B2) and standard M4A3 tank hulls (then called the M36B1). Here, an M36 is photographed in the Ardennes in January 1945.

T67 Gun Motor Carriage. Instead of merely adapting an existing chassis, this was an attempt to design a tank destroyer from basics. It had a similar turret to the M10 prototype, the T35 GMC, but suspension was torsion bar. It mounted a 75 mm gun, as in the Sherman, but this was later changed for a 76 mm on later pilot models which were then redesignated as T70 GMC.

T70 Gun Motor Carriage. The photograph shows one of the six new pilot models, which were identical to the T67 GMC but had the new 76 mm M1 gun in place of the 75 mm. Note the .50 cal Browning on the rear of the TD.

M18 Gun Motor Carriage (*Bottom left*). A good shot of an M18 GMC engaging an enemy target, the dust swirling around as the TD fires, in Wiesloch, Germany, on 1 April 1945. Also called Hellcat, it was very fast, with a top speed of 50–55 mph. Its low silhouette and good cross country performance made it liked by the crews.

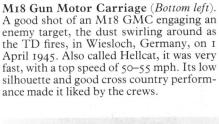

Howitzer Motor Carriage T88. In August 1944 work started on a development of the Hellcat, mounting a 105 mm T12 howitzer on a similar chassis. The pilot model, seen here, was completed in late 1944, but the project was cancelled at the end of the war when the Tank Destroyer Force was disbanded.

World War Two
8 Under New Management

The last part of this photo history of tanks in two world wars deals with some examples of AFVs in service with countries other than the original manufacturers. The first of these is Russia, and although the USSR was a major tank producer in its own right, it still obtained many tanks from both the USA and UK. China, on the other hand, had no tank production of its own and consequently all its tanks had to come from the other three major Allies, Britain, the USA and the USSR.

I have also included France in this part of the history because it would be wrong to discount entirely the part played by French armour during World War 2. As the photographs show, the story really divides itself into three distinct parts. First, there are examples of French tanks in action against the invading German Panzer Divisions in 1940. Sadly, despite the large numbers of tanks available and the soundness of their design, French armoured forces were easily defeated. French manned armour thus disappeared with the fall of France in 1940, but those tanks which had survived the battle – and their numbers were considerable – were put to good use by the victors. The Germans did this with the armour of most other countries they overran, thus

building up quite a galaxy of foreign AFVs. French tanks in service with the Germans included the Char B1 *bis*, Somua and various Hotchkiss models, together with numerous self-propelled guns and howitzers mounted on captured tank chassis. However, Free French armoured forces were formed in 1943–44, the 'Division Blindée' being totally equipped by the United States. Three of these formations took part in the landings on the south coast of France and the 2nd French Armored Division, under General Leclerc, liberated Paris in August 1944, whilst serving as part of General Patton's US Third Army.

French tank design was almost dormant throughout the war years, although some technicians did work in secret during the occupation, on a new heavy tank, the ARL 44, which weighed 48-tons and mounted a 90 mm gun. Some 50 were built after the war but were soon withdrawn from service.

Finally, the tanks of all nations changed hands both on and off the battlefield. In every theatre of war such important weapons could not be allowed to stand around idle and unused for long. As the photographs show, Allied tanks were used by the Axis and vice versa.

This captured Polish TKS tankette, taken during the invasion of
Poland, now has a new driver.

Allied Tanks in Russian and Chinese Service

American tanks in Russia. Large numbers of American tanks were sent to Russia under Lend-Lease, such as these M3 Honey light tanks seen here crossing a river in the Caucasus in October 1942.

British tanks in Russia. A column of British Valentines also in the Caucasus move down a hillside track. It is possible that these were built in Canada and shipped out to Russia under Lend-Lease arrangements. Note that each has an anti-aircraft machine gun fitted.

American tanks in China. Most Chinese equipment used in World War 2 was supplied by the United States, like this M3A3, which was armed with a 37 mm gun.

British tanks in China. China bought a number of Vickers 6-tonners from Great Britain in 1935–36. Two types can be seen here, the Mark E (Type B) and the Mark F. The latter had an extension at the back of the turret to make room for radio equipment. Here, a column of Chinese tank crews await the signal to go into action against the Japanese in Hunan Province.

Russian tanks in China. Chinese tank crews manning Russian-built T26B light tanks pass in review in front of Lung Yun, Governor of Yunan Province in 1944. The three tanks seen in this photograph are all the Commander's model with frame aerials fixed around the turret. Note the Chinese emblem on the front of each tank.

Somewhere in France. Long rows of brand new tanks get ready to leave the factory to be kitted up and taken over by their units. Although the French Army had relatively few new tanks in the early 1930s, production rose sharply to over 2,000 in 1939 and to a total of some 800 medium and 2,700 new tanks by 1940. It is a pity that they were used so badly when the German *Blitzkrieg* swept through France. The tanks seen here are mainly the Renault R35 of which some 2,000 were built, plus a few of the earlier AMC35 which was armed with a 25 mm gun instead of the 37 mm of the R35.

Crews mount! French tank crews rush to mount their Char D2 infantry support tanks during a training exercise. Sadly, the French tactics still mainly tied their tanks to supporting the infantry, deploying them thinly across the battlefield so that they were easy meat for the concentrated German armoured thrusts.

The victors inspect the spoils of war
(*Above*). German soldiers examine an
undamaged Hotchkiss H35 light tank,
captured during the May 1940 campaign.

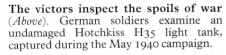

Abandoned! (*Top left*). The fate of so
many French tanks is typified by this
Somua S35, abandoned by its crew. The
Somua was an excellent tank, superior in
armour and firepower to many of its German counterparts.

Conquered! (*Centre left*). An AMC35, its
47 mm gun pointing to the ground, rear
turret exit door open and deserted by its
crew, stands beside the grave of a French
Poilu. France was now in German hands.

Captured! The fate of many French tanks
was to be like these Hotchkiss H39s, namely
pressed into German service. They were
known as the Panzerkampfwagen 38H
735(f), the designation to covering all H35,
H38 and H39 French tanks captured. Certain modifications were made before issue;
for example, the commander's cupola was
removed and replaced by a split hatch.

Victory! (*Above*). Back in French hands an R35 light tank takes part in a triumphal parade in front of Allied officers.

Free French (*Top left*). This Char D1 infantry tank was fortunately serving in North Africa in May 1940, so avoiding capture. It was used against the Germans after the Allied 'Torch' landings in November 1942. Note the tricolour marking on the side.

'France First' (*Centre left*). The Free French Forces were mainly equipped with Allied tanks such as this American light tank M3A3. Note that as well as the tricolour, now much smaller, the tank carries a large new national identification symbol with red/blue top and bottom corners and white centre plus the words *FRANCE D'ABORD*.

Revenge! An elderly Char B1-bis gets its own back on the Germans during the liberation of Paris in August 1944. Note the symbol FFI (*Forces Français Interieur*) prominently displayed on the side and turret.

Captured Tanks

Vingt Ans Plus Tard. Even World War 1 vintage tanks were not to be ignored. Elderly French FT18s, now bearing German crosses, were used for internal security operations in France after its fall in 1940. The Germans renamed it the Pzkpfw 18R 730(f).

Blondie. A Churchill Mark III, complete with its new blond Aryan crew.

Beute. A captured Russian T35 heavy tank (Commander's model) is investigated by triumphant German troops. It was probably never used by the Germans as it was inferior to their own AFVs. Later on in the war they did put captured tanks to good use.

Under new management! This Type 95 (Ha Go) was about the best Japanese tank of World War 2. It was captured in the Central Pacific area and used by the Americans.

Indian troops have taken over this Japanese carrier, captured somewhere in Burma, during the advance of the victorious XIVth Army under General Bill Slim.

(*Below left*). An M13/40 Italian medium tank, taken in the Western desert, one of many captured then and pressed into service. For example, the Sixth Australian Cavalry used a mixture of M13/40 and M11/39 to equip three squadrons. The tanks were used in the attack on Tobruk in January 1941 with large white kangaroos painted on the sides, front and turret.

(*Below*). GIs have taken over this late model Stu H42 assault howitzer, with its *Saukopf* (sows head) gun mantlet.

Russian tank men captured this Pzkpfw III Ausf H/J from the Germans during their retreat and then used it against its former owners.

The best of the bunch in this short survey of captured equipment is this German Panther captured in running order by the British on the 2nd Army front.

Index

This book groups tanks by era, country and basic type, so a comprehensive index is superfluous, but, as many are better known by name than type, this index lists these, plus special AFVs.